John Carroll

Project Program and Portfolio Management

in easy steps

In easy steps is an imprint of In Easy Steps Limited
16 Hamilton Terrace · Holly Walk · Leamington Spa
Warwickshire · United Kingdom · CV32 4LY
www.ineasysteps.com

Copyright © 2014 by In Easy Steps Limited. All rights reserved. No part
of this book may be reproduced or transmitted in any form or by any
means, electronic or mechanical, including photocopying, recording,
or by any information storage or retrieval system, without prior
written permission from the publisher.

Notice of Liability
Every effort has been made to ensure that this book contains accurate
and current information. However, In Easy Steps Limited and the
author shall not be liable for any loss or damage suffered by readers
as a result of any information contained herein.

Trademarks
All trademarks are acknowledged as belonging to their respective
companies.

In Easy Steps Limited supports The Forest Stewardship Council (FSC),
the leading international forest certification organisation. All our titles
that are printed on Greenpeace approved FSC certified paper carry the
FSC logo.

MIX
Paper from
responsible sources
FSC® C020837

Printed and bound in the United Kingdom

ISBN 978-1-84078-626-2

Contents

Note from the author

In case you were wondering why there isn't a comma after 'Project' in the title of the book, it's because the book doesn't cover project management, it covers project program management and portfolio management, which are developments from and extensions to project management. A project program refers to a series of projects that are related, and together will achieve a major change in a business. A portfolio refers to the total set of all the projects and programs being carried out in a business at any given time.

Although I have included a chapter on project management, it is not intended to be a complete coverage of the subject. It is only included to establish a baseline from which to compare and contrast program management and portfolio management. For a complete coverage of project management, I would recommend Effective Project Management in easy steps (or Agile Project Management in easy steps, if you are working in an agile project environment).

I have included a high-level road map for implementing program and portfolio management on the inside front cover and a more detailed road map in chapter 11, but this is only a suggested approach and nothing in this book should be considered as mandatory. However, implementing anything as significant as program or portfolio management without first establishing the existing level of project management maturity would introduce a serious level of risk to the process. Otherwise, feel free to cherry pick the bits that apply to your organization.

Acknowledgements

I would like to express my sincere thanks and gratitude to Graham Moore and David Carpenter-Clawson. Two good friends, former colleagues and very experienced project management professionals. Not only for their time and patience in reviewing the drafts of this book but for their valuable input of positive suggestions and ideas.

1 Introduction

This chapter introduces Project Program and Portfolio Management and explains how they can help to ensure successful projects.

Implementing project program and portfolio management (P3M) can bring significant benefits to any organization, whether large or small.

Overview

Project Program and Portfolio Management (P3M) represents project management taken to the enterprise level. It is increasingly being seen as critical for large organizations (such as governments and multinational corporations) but it can also play a significant part in improving the success rate and financial payback from projects in any size or type of organization. But before we get into the details, let us start with a basic definition of each term:

Project

A project can be described as a temporary organization that will focus on the creation of a set of business deliverables (as defined by the project scope), within an agreed time span (usually of a year or less), cost budget and quality parameters. A project will be justified by its business case and will deliver some form of new product, service, system or business process.

Projects are generally well-defined although they can also be complicated. Their focus is to provide changes that are needed in the business now.

Program

A project program (usually just referred to as a program) again refers to a temporary organization but this one will coordinate, direct and oversee the implementation of a series of related projects and supporting activities to deliver outcomes and benefits in line with the organization's strategic objectives. Programs are the link between the business strategy and the individual projects that will implement the solutions required to deliver it.

Programs are generally complex and will deliver multiple products and services aligned to the business strategy. They will usually span several years and therefore the scope, time and cost are likely to change during the life of a program.

Portfolio

A portfolio refers to the total set of programs, stand alone projects and other change initiatives undertaken by an organization. It is aligned to the organization's budgetary and decision making processes and is the link between the corporate and business strategy and the programs and projects that will deliver it.

Portfolios have strategic corporate deliverables and are on-going. They are reviewed and revised regularly and changed as needed.

The following diagram illustrates the relationship between corporate and business strategy, portfolios, programs and projects:

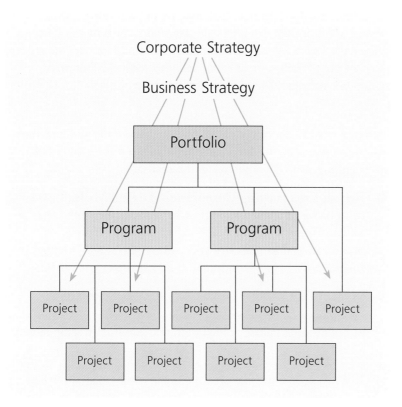

Corporate strategy is implemented through the business strategy and the portfolio is aligned with the business strategy. The business strategy is then implemented through the programs and projects that make up the portfolio. Portfolio management ensures that all projects and programs stay aligned with the business strategy and deliver business benefits. Program management also ensures that projects deliver business benefits.

Who This Book is For

There are many books on project management but far fewer on program and portfolio management. The few books that have been published tend to be theoretical or technical, rather than hands on guides. This book is for people who will be commissioning, running or involved in the delivery of project programs or portfolios and who need to get up to speed quickly on P3M.

Hot tip

This book explains how to implement effective project program and portfolio management (P3M) in any organization and in easy steps.

Leviathans and Vanities

The reason we need P3M stems from the fact that the majority of organizations have a poor record when it comes to delivering business change projects. According to most surveys, around 25% of projects are total failures and have to be abandoned, while around another 50% are seriously late, way over budget or fail to deliver the full business requirements. But there are two specific types of projects that most often seem to result in failure or significant wasted effort: Leviathans and vanities.

Leviathans

Leviathans were enormous, mythical all-consuming sea monsters which sounds awfully like some of the recent high-profile failed or struggling projects reported in the media:

- **British Broadcasting Corporation: Digital Media Initiative**, to improve efficiency and allow better management, but underestimation of the complexity, poor governance, organizational immaturity and continual changes resulted in the contract being abandoned in 2013, at a cost of £100m.

- **State of California: 21st Century Project (MyCalPAYS)** payroll and benefits system development. After eight months of operational failures the system was eventually scrapped, at a cost of around $254m.

- **BSkyB: Customer Relations Management system**, where the supplier failed to resource the project properly and was seriously late. When the project was finally scrapped, little had been accomplished but the cost was £318m.

- **UK Government Regional Fire Control Centre project**, which was flawed from the outset and scrapped as the IT systems could not be delivered. The cost was £469m at the time of cancellation but the costs are still on-going.

- **US Department of Defense: Expeditionary Combat Support System (ECSS)**, an integrated supply chain and logistics system (at one time the largest project in the world), finally scrapped as they couldn't get it to work at a cost of $1b.

- **Airbus SAS: A380 commercial aircraft development project**, delayed by nearly two years due to design faults caused by the use of different computer aided design (CAD) software in different parts of the organization at a cost of $6b.

The problem with these Leviathan projects is they become like out of control giant tankers, almost impossible to stop until they hit a rock and flounder. Many more projects end up like this than get reported in the media; they get hushed up by the embarrassed organizations responsible for them.

So what can we learn from them? Effective Project Management in easy steps (a companion volume to this book) defines 20 laws of project management. The most pertinent of these is this:

> *"A two year project will take three years;*
> *a three year project will never finish."*

The basic problem is that the world will change, often quite dramatically, over a two to three year period. As a result of this, the business requirements are also likely to change in line with it. With the passage of time, what the project initially set out to achieve will no longer be what the business now requires.

Changing the project's requirements (scope) on the fly will seriously impact on the project's time, cost and quality. This will add to the risk of it falling further and further behind until, eventually, it gets abandoned. The larger the project is, the greater the risk of failure.

Beware

There is a direct correlation between the size of a project and its risk of failure.

Vanities

The second type of problem projects are vanity projects, promoted by proud men (usually senior executives) with whom no-one likes to disagree. These typically have poorly defined objectives and no sound business justification. They may eventually get completed but they produce little or no real benefit to the business despite using precious resources. Even worse, they prevent those resources being used for projects of more value to the business.

The problem is that without proper project, program and portfolio management processes in place each individual project is considered in isolation. It doesn't matter if the project is necessary or not, as long as the person sponsoring it can make a convincing case for it. In fact it might not even need corporate approval if the sponsor has sufficient finance in his own budget to fund it.

So clearly what is needed is some process for screening out these Leviathan and vanity projects and that process is what P3M is all about delivering.

Hot tip

It might be thought that hosting the Olympics or Football World Cup can tick both of these boxes!

A Cautionary Tale

Once Upon a Time

Many years ago, while working as a project manager for a fairly large manufacturing company, I took up a new position based at the organization's headquarters. While being given a tour of the site, I was proudly shown the shiny new mainframe computer system they had recently bought. I discovered fairly quickly that the beast was hardly used and had masses of spare capacity but it took me a little longer to find out the story behind its purchase.

The head of information technology had proposed it as he wanted to have the biggest and best computer to impress other heads of information technology. He also had the support of the chief finance officer, who had been lavishly wined and dined by the suppliers. Aided by a brilliant presentation from the supplier's top sales executive, they pitched their proposal to the board of directors. To say that the board was baffled by science would have been an understatement but they felt happy that the head of IT and CFO must have understood it as they were proposing it.

The business case (developed and presented by the supplier) had some very big numbers in it. Although the computer was expensive, it looked like the payback would also be enormous, through impressive cost savings, huge cash flow benefits and some exciting new opportunities. Of course, the details of the savings and new opportunities were not presented (they didn't want to bore the board with details) and rumor has it they never existed. Needless to say, after an hour of high-pressure sales pitch the board agreed it on the nod. Exit one very happy head of IT and a salesman already thinking of how he would spend his not insubstantial commission.

The Punch Line

The next item on the agenda was repainting the bicycle shed and this the board did understand. Indeed they argued for hours about what color it should be and where the cheapest paint could be purchased. But when they finally finished the meeting they felt they had done a good day's work.

Does that sound unbelievable? Well to tell the truth I did borrow the bit about the bike shed but the rest is real and I saw it almost happen again a few years later at another business. Is that any way to make business decisions about major projects and gain real competitive advantage for a business?

The decision as to which projects should go ahead is far too often based on the organizational clout of the person sponsoring or proposing the project. Many organizations do try to allocate funds to projects that are perceived as adding the most value to the business. But unless there are mature business processes in place to support the decision making and subsequent monitoring of the resultant projects, they can still end up as Leviathans or vanities.

What Business Benefits?

Even apart from these Leviathan and vanity projects, the general failure rate of all business change projects is still way too high (as detailed on page 10). Without established P3M practices in place the majority of projects still do not satisfy the basic criteria of being on time, to budget and to scope (referred to as the iron triangle). What's worse, nearly three-quarters of organizations do not even bother to evaluate and report on these project variations.

If that wasn't bad enough, of the projects that do get completed, around 70% do not deliver the business benefits that were promised for them. The vast majority of organizations do not track the actual benefits realized to the business, so have no way of even knowing whether or not they justified the business case they were based on. This is referred to as authorize and forget!

Fear of Failure

There is another factor that makes the situation even worse. Part way through a project it is not unusual for the project team to realize that the promised business benefits are unlikely to be realized, but there is an organizational fear about canceling projects as it is seen as failure and no one likes to be associated with a failure. So the project stumbles blindly on.

Project Overlap

One final factor is that projects do not often happen in complete isolation. There are frequently other projects taking place which could have an impact on them. If there is no mechanism in place to coordinate projects and no regular channel for inter-project communications, projects can have an adverse impact on, or totally nullify the work of other projects.

The good news is that properly implemented P3M can and will address all of these problems and ensure a much higher rate of general project success with far fewer total failures.

Beware

If an organization is not tracking and recording the results of projects, they will never improve their rate of success.

13

Hot tip

In the next topic we will see how P3M can solve these types of problems.

How P3M Can Help

Some major research carried out for the government of New Zealand in 2007 also studied project management practices in the USA, UK, Canada and Australia. It found that there was not only a significant opportunity for increasing the success rate and reducing the cost of projects by using P3M, but also that poorly defined or low payback projects were much more likely to be scrapped with P3M in place.

Overall, the research found that the amount of benefits leakage (benefits promised in a project's business case, which the project fails to deliver), could be reduced by a quarter to a half with P3M. They also found that it resulted in far fewer complete failures in organizations that had implemented it.

So how can P3M help with Leviathan projects, vanity projects and failed projects in general?

Enter the Program

Starting with the large (Leviathan) projects, the solution is to break these down into smaller sub-projects (preferably of no more than one year's duration), each of which will achieve some of the prioritized business requirements. Each of these sub-projects should then be treated as a project in its own right and project managed accordingly.

The development of agile project methods, which can deliver prioritized business requirements much faster than traditional methods, can then also be utilized where appropriate. However, these sub-projects, together with any temporary operational and support procedures, are still related and need to be managed as a coherent group and that group is a program.

But this will still leave most organizations with a number of projects and now programs competing for scarce human and financial resources.

Enter the Portfolio

By treating the totality of the organization's programs and projects as a single portfolio, they can be ranked on their alignment with corporate strategy and their potential business benefits.

Supported and reinforced by a number of other processes such as project office and authorization gateways, portfolio management optimizes the organization's projects and programs, so that only

Beware

Surveys have identified that the risk of project failure increases dramatically once the duration exceeds a year.

the most beneficial are authorized to proceed. It also ensures that those that do go ahead have a much greater chance of success.

Project Success

The portfolio and programs are still implemented through a number of individual projects. But with P3M there will be effective and mature project management processes in place which of themselves will reduce the likelihood of project failure. The implementation of P3M will help to ensure that:

- Only the most appropriate projects are commissioned in line with corporate strategy

- All projects will deliver value for the organization

- There is a proper monitoring of return on investment

- More projects are successful, there is less wasted effort and there are far fewer total failures

Can Methodologies Help?

A number of methodologies, standards and practices for P3M have been developed in recent years. The principal ones are those from the Project Management Institute (PMI) in the USA and the Office of Government Commerce (OGC) in the UK.

PMI first issued their Project Management Body of Knowledge (PMBOK) as a white paper in 1983 and have subsequently developed that methodology together with their Standard for Program Management and Standard for Portfolio Management.

OGC has taken a similar role and first issued PRINCE (Projects in Controlled Environments) in 1989. This was further developed and relaunched as PRINCE2 in 1996 and they have since added Managing Successful Programmes, Management of Portfolios and Gateway Reviews.

Potentially of more benefit, although not a methodology, is the Capability Maturity Model (CMM) developed by the Software Engineering Institute (SEI) at Carnegie Mellon University. Both PMI and OGC have also developed models based on it.

This book indicates the potential advantages of each methodology and where they can usefully be applied. However, none of these methodologies are essential for the introduction of P3M.

Hot tip

While methodologies can help, this book also provides an independent route to the implementation of P3M based on best practice.

How the Book is Organized

The rest of the book will expand on projects, programs, portfolios and the management of them. It will also look at creating the right business infrastructure to support them and how to make the best use of the organization's resources. You can work your way through the book from cover to cover, but if you want to home in on a particular subject the following sections explain what each chapter covers.

Setting the Scene

Chapter 2 provides a brief overview of project management and how it differs from operational management. This provides a baseline against which to compare program and portfolio management in the following chapters. It covers what project management involves, methodologies, project life cycle, project management maturity and the role of the project office.

Chapter 3 introduces program management and explains how it differs from project management. It describes the interface between a program and its constituent projects. It also covers benefits management, stakeholder management, program governance, the program life cycle, program controls, program management maturity and the role of the program office.

Chapter 4 introduces portfolio management, portfolio selection, the portfolio life-cycle and portfolio management maturity. It focuses on the interface between it, corporate strategy and the programs and projects that will implement the portfolio.

Preparing the Organization

Chapter 5 examines the business environment in which the projects, programs and portfolios are executed and what is required to support them. It looks at the importance of organizational capability maturity and the process of developing that maturity. Finally, it explains how a properly established project, program and portfolio office can support the process.

Implementing Program Management

Chapter 6 explains how to go about implementing program management in an organization. It sets out the precursors that must be in place, the required level of project management maturity, establishing a program office, program governance, the program organization and the key processes that need to be in place to support it.

Chapter 7 examines what's involved in managing a program through the program life cycle. It explains what is required in each phase and each stage from preparation and initiation, through setting up a program infrastructure and benefits delivery to program closure and transition.

Implementing Portfolio Management

Chapters 8 explains how to go about implementing portfolio management in an organization. It explains the precursors and level of organizational maturity required to support it. It expands on the role of the portfolio office, portfolio governance, the portfolio organization and the key processes required to support it.

Chapter 9 examines what is involved in managing a portfolio through the portfolio definition and delivery life cycle. It explains what is needed in the six processes of: portfolio selection, portfolio prioritization, portfolio planning, benefits management, risk management and stakeholder management.

Gateway Reviews

Chapter 10 looks at the gateway review process and how it can help to exercise improved governance of programs and large projects. It covers the six gateways (phase and stage reviews): strategic investment, benefits justification, delivery strategy, investment decision, readiness for service and benefits realization.

Implementation

Chapter 11 sets out a road map for the successful introduction of project, program and portfolio management. This road map and action plan really do work as the author has used them successfully in a number of organizations. It will be an exciting journey and the benefits it will bring are:

- Projects will perform better and better as the organization's capability maturity develops

- Program management brings a better use of resources and a focus on changes that will deliver real benefits

- Gateway reviews ensure that programs and projects are effective and unnecessary projects don't take place

- Portfolio management puts control right back where it should be at the strategic heart of the business

Summary

- Project, Program and Portfolio Management (P3M) should be considered critical for any large organization and can play a significant part in improving the success rate and financial payback from projects in any size or type of organization

- Projects should be short (a year or less) and focus on changes needed in the business right now

- Programs are longer-term collections of related projects and other activities that will be managed in a coordinated way

- Portfolio refers to the total set of programs and projects being undertaken by the organization and managed in line with corporate strategy

- Large (Leviathan) projects are better managed by being broken down into smaller sub-projects and then managed as a program of projects

- Vanity projects will typically have poorly defined objectives and no sound business justification

- Unless there are mature management processes in place to support the decision making and subsequent monitoring of projects, they can still end up as failures

- Fear of canceling failing projects (no one likes to be seen as failing) can result in them stumbling blindly on

- Projects do not often happen in isolation, there will be other projects going on that could be impacted by or have an impact on them

- The decision as to which projects should go ahead should be based on their alignment to the strategy of the organization and their perceived ability to add value to the business

- Program and portfolio management can help to ensure that the most appropriate projects are commissioned in line with corporate strategy and that more projects are successful

- There are a number of methodologies that can provide useful starting points for the development of organizational standards and methods, but they are not essential

2 Project Management

This chapter summarizes the management of projects and sets a baseline for explaining how program and portfolio management differ from it in subsequent chapters.

Projects

Projects and programs (we will get onto portfolios later) and therefore project and program management are frequently confused with one another. The simplest way of avoiding this confusion is to think of programs as 'project programs', that is to say programs of projects. So a program consists of a number of projects. The purpose of this chapter is to provide a basic definition of projects and project management so that later chapters can build on this in defining programs and portfolios and how the management of them differs from and interrelates with project management.

What is a Project?

To start at the very beginning, a project is simply a series of tasks or activities that have to be carried out in order to bring about a change or achieve some other identified objective. The project could be a personal one such as writing a book on project, program and portfolio management, a construction project like building a house, or it could be to implement a new business venture. The results of the project are often referred to as the product, which is effectively what is left in place once the project has been successfully completed.

What a project is not is business as usual, that is defined as operations and is covered in a later topic (on page 24). A project will, however, result in a change to an operational process or a brand new operational process, in either case resulting in a new or revised business as usual.

Project Characteristics

Whatever type of project it is, there are three key characteristics that can be associated with it:

1. It must have a goal (some sort of specific outcome or objective), as there would be no point in carrying out a project if it did not achieve anything of benefit

2. It must be started or initiated, as projects do not usually happen spontaneously

3. It needs someone (the project manager) to run it and steer it through to achievement of the goal

So a project is the implementation of a change, with a beginning, middle and an end. It will also have a finite time frame, it will be unique (every project is different in some way), people are involved and it will usually have finite resources (people, time and money). The following diagram illustrates a typical project life cycle for a five stage project:

Start Up				Close Down
Initiation	Stage	Stage	Stage	Implementation

Projects are split up into a number of stages for control purposes and can have anything from three to as many as eight or nine stages. They can vary in size from a very small project carried out by just one person (perhaps a process change project) to large projects involving many people from different parts of the organization and even other organizations.

The beginning, middle and end stages of a project all have their own characteristics. Traditionally, the first stage is called the initiation stage, as it gets the project initiated or started up. The final stage of the project is typically called the implementation stage, which includes closing the project down and learning from it. The middle stages will usually be named after the main activity in the stage such as design or build.

Projects will usually result in ongoing operations and, like operations, they will also involve processes. Operations and processes are covered in two later topics.

Closing a Project
Normally the end and close down of a project will happen when the project has met its objectives and delivered the required product or service. However a project can also be terminated before it has been successfully completed for a variety of reasons. Typically, a project would be terminated because the product is no longer required or it has proved too costly to justify implementing it. Whatever the reason for closing a project it should go through a formal, documented closure process to capture any lessons learned for the organization.

Hot tip

Capturing lessons learned is an essential step in improving project management in any organization.

Project Management

Simply stated, the role of the project manager is to deliver the project on time, within budget and with the needs of the business fully met. However, that is by no means a full description of project management.

Whatever the objectives of the project are, they will involve some change to the business, so project management is the management of change. The project manager requires all the basic management skills together with the ability to manage change. These are some of the key things that the project manager will need to do:

1 **Clarify the Objectives:** projects often start out with poorly defined objectives, these need to be clarified and agreed with management

2 **Develop the Plan:** planning is probably the single most important activity a project manager has to carry out and it is ongoing for the duration of the project

3 **Manage and Motivate the Team:** although they do not usually have line management responsibility, they still have to keep the team managed and motivated

4 **Manage the Risks:** change always involves risks and these risks are compounded by the uncertainty and unknowns that exist at the start of a project

5 **Deal with Problems:** problems will occur and the project manager needs to plan for them and deal with them

6 **Measure Progress:** the project manager needs an accurate way of measuring project progress against the plan

7 **Communicate:** the project team and other stakeholders need to know what's happening on a project

8 **Steer the Project to Completion:** the project manager also has to retain the big picture and make sure the project stays on track to its destination

Project Management Skills

There are four key skills that a project manager needs in order to be effective:

- **Planning:** a lack of adequate planning is the single most common cause of project failure

- **Organizing:** making sure everything happens when it needs to and not too soon or too late

- **Leading:** the people working on the project together with all the other project stakeholders

- **Controlling:** to measure and report on progress, identify risks, issues and problems and deal with them

Plus the ability to communicate effectively in order to keep all the stakeholders fully in the picture.

Project Management Characteristics

To enable a later comparison with program management, we can now define a number of characteristics for project management:

- **Change:** project managers try to minimize changes to the scope of a project

- **Leadership Style:** project managers tend to focus on getting team members to complete their allocated work

- **Management Skills:** project managers are team players who need to use their skills and knowledge to motivate the team

- **Monitoring:** project managers monitor and control the project tasks in order to get the project deliverables produced

- **People Management:** project managers usually have no direct authority over the team and need to use influencing skills

- **Planning:** project managers are responsible for creating and maintaining detailed plans for their projects

- **Scope:** a project typically has a narrow scope limited to delivering its product or results

- **Success:** project management success is measured by whether the project is completed on time, to budget and to scope

Beware

Making someone a project manager who does not have these basic management skills can result in serious problems.

Beware

Even when a project is delivered on time, to budget and scope; it can still be a disaster if any of the stakeholders' needs and interests are ignored.

Operations

Projects are needed to carry out activities that cannot be addressed using the normal ongoing operations of the organization. To establish whether an undertaking is a project or not, we need to understand the differences between a project and an operation.

An ongoing operation is a set of tasks that do not have a beginning or an end. If a department in the organization produces widgets, they will carry on performing the same set of tasks to produce those widgets year after year.

If a new improved way of making widgets is discovered then the operation needs to be changed and the employees retrained. That change process is a project and its product will be the new operational process.

The product life cycle (as illustrated on the right) begins with a project to develop and implement a new product and bring it into operational service. It will continue in operational service (perhaps with occasional enhancement or maintenance) until it is no longer required or is to be replaced with a new product. It will then be decommissioned.

Projects and operations do, however, share a large number of characteristics:

- Both have objectives for what is to be produced

- Both require people to carry out the work together with a budget for the resources used

- Both require the work to be planned and tasks to be allocated

- Both require leadership

- Both require the output from tasks to be monitored and feedback given to the people producing them

The real distinction between projects and operations is that a project is temporary and unique while an operation is ongoing and repetitive.

Hot tip

Enhancement, maintenance and decommissioning of the product should all be carried out as projects.

24

Product Life Cycle
Project
Operational Service
Decommission

Processes

Project management (like operations management) is performed through a series of processes. Processes can be anything from opening and distributing mail to building a new airport. However, simple or complex, all processes have three elements: input, process and output, as illustrated in the following IPO diagram:

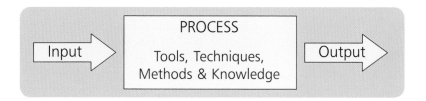

This IPO process model is sometimes extended to a SIPOC: Supplier>Input> Process>Output> Consumer model.

Input
The input to a process is the raw material or data needed to start the process. The mail, specification or blueprints in the examples above. It would also include the list of tasks or activities to be performed and the deliverables required.

Process
The actual process itself consists of the tools, techniques and methods that will be used to turn the raw input into the required output. For example, project scheduling software in developing plans and schedules. The process could also require work estimating guidelines and standards, together with skills and knowledge in the people carrying out the work.

Output
The output is the result of the process and will consist of one or more tangible deliverables. This would include the project plan and schedule in the above example.

Different processes will be needed at different stages in a project. In early stages, processes such as defining the objectives and planning the work will be needed. In the middle stages, the actual work of the project will be performed and progress monitored. Towards the end of the project the new operational processes will be implemented and the project closed down.

The project life cycle defines the project in terms of the number of stages and the purpose of each. Each stage will then consist of a number of processes. We will look at two project management methodologies and how they address this in the next topic.

PRINCE

The two most widely used project management methodologies are PMBOK (covered in the next topic) and PRINCE.

PRINCE

Projects in Controlled Environments (PRINCE) is a generic methodology that can be applied to any project. It consists of seven principles, seven themes and seven processes, together with advice on tailoring the methodology to suit the project.

Principles

The seven principles, developed from lessons learned over a number of years, provide a framework of good practice:

- The project should have continued business justification

- The project team should learn from experience

- Roles and responsibilities for the team should be defined

- The project should be managed stage by stage

- Management by exception, within defined tolerances

- Focus on the delivery of products (deliverables)

- Tailor the method to suit the project size and complexity

Themes

The seven themes represent the aspects of project management that need to be continually monitored throughout the project life cycle. They contain guidance on how the process should be performed, setting baselines and how progress should be monitored and controlled. The themes are:

- **Business Case:** the justification for the project

- **Organization:** the people in the project and their roles

- **Quality:** how quality is defined and assured

- **Plans:** what plans will be produced and when

- **Risk:** how risk will be managed on the project

- **Change:** how change will be assessed and authorized

- **Progress:** how progress will be monitored and controlled

Process Model

The PRINCE processes model defines seven processes (illustrated in blue), which define the way project activities are carried out, how they interrelate and how they are controlled:

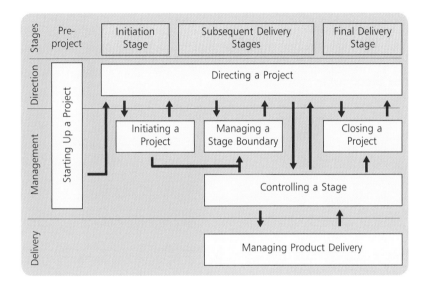

The seven processes are:

- **Directing a Project:** the project board exercise control of the project, while delegating management to the project manager

- **Starting up a Project:** the pre-project processes required to bring a project into existence and gain corporate approval

- **Initiating a Project:** production of the project plan, strategy and controls (documented in the project initiation document)

- **Controlling a Stage:** allocation of work, progress monitoring, identifying risks and issues, reporting and communication

- **Managing Product Delivery:** the processes required to supervise the detailed work of producing the deliverables

- **Managing a Stage Boundary:** reporting project progress and requesting authorization to start the next stage

- **Closing a Project:** to confirm project acceptance, hand over and decommissioning

PMBOK

Perhaps the most widely used project management methodology is the Project Management Body of Knowledge (PMBOK). Strictly speaking, it is defined as a project management standard but is in practice a methodology. It can be applied to any size or type of project and is widely used throughout the world.

Process Model

The PMBOK process model (as illustrated below) has five project process groups supported by nine knowledge areas which define the processes in more detail.

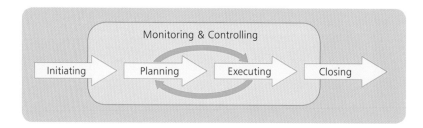

The five project process groups are:

- **Initiating:** the project is authorized, the project manager appointed, the project charter produced, the business case documented and the outline project plan produced

- **Planning:** the objectives and requirements are refined, the project management plan is developed, the project scope statement is produced and stage plans are developed

- **Executing:** the work required to meet the plans is carried out and the main deliverables of the project are produced together with any approved changes

- **Monitoring and Controlling:** progress and performance are monitored, change requests and defects are identified and subjected to an appropriate change control process

- **Closing:** formal acceptance of the project product, hand over to the operations and maintenance groups, the project is reviewed and any recommendations are documented

The middle three process groups are carried out continuously and seamlessly during each of the middle stages of the project.

Knowledge Areas

The nine knowledge areas and the processes and activities required to complete them are:

- **Integration Management:** the processes and activities needed for developing the project charter and project management plan, directing and managing project execution, and monitoring and controlling project work.

- **Scope Management:** the processes to collect project requirements, define and control the project scope, and create the work breakdown structure.

- **Time Management:** the processes required to define and sequence activities, estimate activity resources and durations, and develop and control the schedule.

- **Cost Management:** the processes involved in estimating, budgeting and controlling costs so that the project can be completed within the approved budget.

- **Project Quality Management:** the processes required to determine quality policies, objectives and responsibilities including quality assurance and quality control.

- **Human Resource Management:** the processes that organize, manage and lead the project team. This includes developing the human resource plan, acquiring the project team, developing the project team and managing the project team.

- **Communications Management:** the processes required to identify project stakeholders, plan communications, distribute information, manage stakeholder expectations and report performance.

- **Risk Management:** the processes required for planning risk management, identifying risks, performing risk analysis, planning risk responses and monitoring and controlling risks.

- **Procurement Management:** the processes necessary for planning, conducting, administering and closing contracts and supplier relationships.

We will examine how both the PRINCE and PMBOK process models map onto a typical project life cycle in the next topic.

Effective Project Management in easy steps covers the complete project life cycle in detail. From the right way to start a project through to closing it down.

Project Life Cycle

Project management involves managing the project throughout its life cycle, using the relevant processes that make up the project management knowledge areas. It is not essential to use a methodology such as PMBOK or PRINCE to run a project, although many organizations choose to do so.

If we look at a typical five-stage project life cycle (from Effective Project Management in easy steps) we can then see how these two methodologies (and most others) will map onto it:

Start Up				Close Down
Initiation	Strategy	Analysis	Design and Build	Implementation

Start Up: (pre-project) to produce the terms of reference, select the project manager and team and plan the initiation stage.

1 **Initiation Stage:** to confirm the business case, plan the project and produce the project charter

2 **Strategy Stage:** to determine the strategic business requirements and agree them with management

3 **Analysis Stage:** to identify what will have to be done to meet the business requirements

4 **Design and Build Stage:** to design how the business requirements will be met and then build or buy the necessary products, processes and systems to do it

5 **Implementation Stage:** to bring the new products and processes into use, train the staff who will be using them and provide initial support during the cut over

Close Down: following the implementation stage (or included at the end of it) the project will be closed down and formally transferred to operational management.

This typical project life cycle is applicable to most projects of up to one year's duration. However, longer projects would usually require further stages or splitting into phases (covered below). We can now examine how each of the two example methodologies fits with this typical project life cycle:

PRINCE

The PRINCE process model (on page 27) shows the project stages at the top of the model with the processes below. Looking at the five stage life cycle opposite, the mapping is as follows:

- Pre-project start up is exactly the same

- Initiation stage is exactly the same

- Strategy, analysis and design and build stages are all subsequent delivery stages in PRINCE

- Implementation is the final delivery stage in PRINCE

- Close down takes place at the end of the final delivery stage in PRINCE

PMBOK

The PMBOK process model (on page 28) illustrates the five process groups which map onto the five stage project life cycle opposite as follows:

- The initiating process group maps onto the start up and initiation stage

- The planning, executing and monitoring and controlling process groups map onto each of the five stages

- The closing processes group maps onto close down

As can be seen from the above, there is no conflict between the different methodologies and a typical project life cycle, it is just that they are illustrated in different ways and some of the stages and processes are given different names.

Project Phases

Larger projects or projects being run as agile projects will usually be broken down into a number of phases. In this case each phase of the project will still consist of the same stages and processes.

Capability Maturity

The Capability Maturity Model (CMM) was originally developed at Carnegie Mellon University to assess an organization's software engineering maturity. This was then adapted in a number of related areas including project management and redefined as the Capability Maturity Model Integration (CMMI) process. This can be used to guide process improvement across a project, a division or an entire organization.

Capability Maturity Model

The CMM consists of a set of five structured levels that describe how well the organization's behaviors, practices and processes can reliably and sustainably produce the desired outcomes. In this instance, the organization's project management processes.

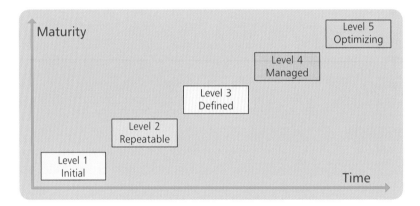

The model involves five aspects:

- **Maturity Levels:** the five levels of process maturity (illustrated above), where the top level represents the ideal state

- **Key Process Areas:** groups of related activities that, when performed together, achieve a set of goals

- **Goals:** the states that must exist for each key process area to have been implemented in an effective and lasting way

- **Common Features:** practices that implement a key process area such as activities performed or measurement, analysis and verification of implementation

- **Key Practices:** the elements that contribute most effectively to the implementation and institutionalization of the area

CMM Levels

The five levels define the predictability, effectiveness and control of an organization's project management processes, which improve as the organization moves up these levels.

The model provides a theoretical continuum along which process maturity can be developed incrementally from one level to the next. Skipping a level is neither allowed nor feasible. The five levels are defined as:

1 **Initial:** at this level project management processes are typically undocumented and in a chaotic or unstable state, tending to be driven in an ad hoc, uncontrolled and reactive manner by users or events

2 **Repeatable:** some project management processes are now documented and repeatable, possibly with consistent results, but process discipline is not rigorous

3 **Defined:** project management processes are defined and documented and subject to some degree of improvement over time, they are used to establish consistency across the entire organization

4 **Managed:** project management processes are established and managed using process metrics and can be adapted to particular projects without measurable losses of quality or deviations from specifications

5 **Optimizing:** at this level the focus is on continually improving process performance through incremental and innovative changes

Organizational Maturity

Any organization considering implementing program or portfolio management must start from at least a stable, managed level of project management maturity. One of the key functions in establishing this is the control of process documentation. This is typically done through the establishment of a project office, which is covered in the next topic.

Project Office

Project office (sometimes called project management office), is a group or department that defines and maintains standards for project management within an organization. The project office is tasked with standardizing and introducing economies of repetition in the execution of projects. It provides the source of documentation, guidance and metrics on project management and the execution of projects.

Why Have a Project Office?

According to the 2009 Standish CHAOS Report, only 32% of projects were completed on time, within budget and delivered measurable business benefits. A PwC survey around the same time found that inadequate estimating accounted for 30% of project failures, lack of executive sponsorship for 16% and poorly defined goals and objectives another 12%. The same survey found that using established project management processes increased success in terms of quality, scope, schedule, budgets and benefits. The survey concluded that operating a project office is one of the top three reasons that drives successful project delivery.

Functions

Project offices may take on a range of functions including:

- Introducing processes and developing suitable standards and methodology

- Selecting, introducing and monitoring the use of software and other tools

- Design training programs to increase the efficiency of project team members

- Allocating pooled resources to project teams

- Providing implementation support and guidance to project managers

- Monitoring and reporting project progress to management and making recommendations on which projects to continue and which to cancel

- Mentoring project team members

- Auditing a project's conformance to project management standards and guidelines and collecting lessons learned

● Conducting project health checks to assess the likelihood of success and recommending remedial action where necessary

Implementation

Setting up a project office is a fairly straightforward process involving the following steps:

1 Obtain management approval and support for the establishment of a project office

2 Define and document the organization's project management standards, methodologies, project life cycle and lessons learned (involving existing project managers)

3 Appoint one or more people (as necessary) to maintain the documentation and filing system and communicate with the project managers

4 Provide any training required to the project office staff in order to enable them to carry out their role

5 Provide any training required by the project managers in the use of the project office documentation and the role of the project office

6 Set up regular process reviews between the project office and project managers, to ensure the development and improvement of standards and methods

Hot tip

A set of checklists for implementing project, program and portfolio office is available on our website. Go to **www.ineasysteps. com/resource-centre/ downloads/**

Management Support

As mentioned in step one above, management approval for setting up the project office is not enough by itself, it is also essential that management fully supports and is ready to enforce the standards and methods where necessary.

The project office can then define best practice, establish and update standard methodology, arrange project team training, provide assistance to projects, provide resources to projects, provide project assurance, project reporting to management and participate in project meetings.

Summary

- Simply stated the role of the project manager is to deliver a project on time, within budget and with the needs of the business fully met

- Project management is the management of change and there are four key project management skills: planning, organizing, leading and controlling; these together with communications form the core of the project management role

- While project management is the management of change, operations management is the ongoing management of the business (sometimes referred to as business as usual)

- There are many similarities between project management and operations management and both are carried out through management processes which require some form of input and produce some form of output

- Projects are carried out in stages, each of which will require a number of processes to be carried out producing a range of outputs (project deliverables)

- PRINCE and PMBOK are the two most widely used project management methodologies and both provide a full set of project management processes for carrying out each stage of a project's life cycle

- A typical project life cycle consists of around five discrete stages and can be carried out using PRINCE, PMBOK or any other form of project management methodology or processes defined by the organization

- Capability maturity is a way of defining an organization's project management processes as one of five levels: Initial (ad-hoc chaotic), Repeatable (some processes are documented), Defined (processes are defined, documented and subject to improvement), Managed (processes are established, measurable and adaptable) or Optimizing (continuous process improvement through incremental and innovative change)

- Project Office is a group or department that is set up to manage the project management processes and supporting material in an organization

3 Program Management

This chapter introduces programs and program management and explains how they differ from projects and project management. It covers four key management themes and the important role of the program office.

Programs

We looked at the basic concepts of project management in the previous chapter, so let's begin this chapter with two definitions:

Program

A program consists of a dossier of related projects and activities, managed in a coordinated fashion in order to deliver outcomes and benefits related to the organization's strategic objectives that would not be available by managing each project individually.

Program Management

Program management is the coordinated management of a program in order to achieve its strategic objectives and deliver strategic benefits to the organization.

There are a number of reasons why an organization might want to run a program, rather than a series of projects, and the two most common are:

1. The organization finds it has a number of strategic projects, which are related to or have an impact on each other, which could be grouped into a single program for better overall control

2. The organization has a large and unwieldy project, which is difficult to control and could be better treated as a program and broken down into a number of smaller and more manageable projects

To be worth considering an initiative as a program, with the greater overheads that involves, the initiative will need to:

- Meet some strategic requirement so that it can be aligned to the organization's strategy

- Enable the realization of benefits; because quantifiable business benefits are the way programs are measured

- Involve a number of projects and possibly other related support and operational activities

- Have a significant duration; typically a program will run over several years and may be broken down into discrete phases (sometimes referred to as tranches)

Beware

Program management does introduce another layer of management, which may not be appropriate for smaller organizations.

In addition to program management, there are said to be three other 'management themes' that run through a program:

Benefits Management

We have seen that a project is focused on the delivery of a product or service, which has been justified by a business case and is expected to deliver benefits to the business (although these are seldom tracked). A program is focused purely on the realization of these benefits, which therefore need to be managed.

Stakeholder Management

In the same way that a project has its stakeholders, a program will also have its stakeholders. Some may be existing project stakeholders while others may just be program stakeholders. In either case they need to be engaged and managed.

Program Governance

A program will be much larger than a project and be strategically important to the business. It will therefore need some high-level oversight. This should ensure the program's strategic alignment, quality assurance and risk and issue management.

Methodologies

There are two main methodologies for program management: the PMI's Standard for Program Management (SPM) and the OGC's Managing Successful Programs (MSP):

SPM defines program management in terms of five performance domains: program strategy alignment, program governance, program life cycle management, program benefits management and program stakeholder engagement.

MSP defines program management in terms of nine governance themes: program organization, vision, stakeholder engagement, benefits management, blueprint design and delivery, planning and control, the business case, risk and issue management, and quality assurance management.

There is a significant overlap in terms of the two methodologies although they use different terminology. The remainder of this chapter expands on program management and the other three management themes, together with the program life cycle, program controls, capability maturity and program office.

Hot tip

Program management as covered in this book will work with either methodology but takes a less restrictive approach to its implementation.

Program Management

Having examined project management in the previous chapter, we can now consider program management and how it differs from project management. Program management involves managing a program, but as that program consists of a number of projects, then each of those projects will be managed by a project manager.

Program management is not about managing the details of each individual project, but rather about managing the big picture, in order to achieve the strategic objectives and realize the benefits for which the program is designed.

It involves managing the things that the project managers don't manage, such as:

1. The inter-dependencies between the individual projects in the program

2. Prioritizing the issues that arise from different projects

3. The strategic goals and objectives of the organization for which the projects are being executed

4. Realization of benefits from the program

5. Management of the program stakeholders (who are not always project stakeholders)

6. Management of program risks

Benefits of Program Management

From the foregoing view of a program and program management, we can start to see some benefits of the process:

- Optimization of human and other resources over multiple projects in the overall program

- Coordinated management and reduction of risks and issues that could impact on the program

- Consolidation and management of the benefits being delivered by the multiple projects in a program

The following diagram illustrates the relationship between program management, project management and benefits:

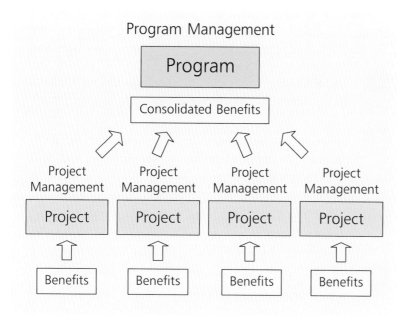

Project Dependencies

Program management involves coordination between the related projects in a program. The projects may be related because they share a common attribute (being performed for the same customer) or because together they will deliver a collective capability or product.

As an example: a large (three year duration) university network upgrade program consisted of two enabling projects (one to replace the entire campus cabling, the other to install new switches, routers and servers) and then one project for the upgrade to each individual building. The later projects were dependant on the enabling projects and inter-dependant for resource allocation.

Program management also involves the other three management themes: benefits management, stakeholder management and program governance. The role of the program manager (and how it differs from the role of a project manager) is explored in the remainder of this topic and the other three management themes are explored in the following three topics.

...cont'd

The Program Manager

The program manager's role is to oversee the projects in the program and provide high level guidance to the project managers. They coordinate efforts between projects, but do not directly manage them, that is still the role of the project managers. The following are the main responsibilities of program management:

1. Identification, monitoring, controlling, and rationalization of the dependencies among the projects in a program

2. Determining which issues among the projects in the program should be escalated to program level and dealing with the escalated issues

3. Identifying any risks to the program and managing those risks

4. Tracking the contribution of each project to the consolidated program benefits

5. Tracking the contribution of any non-project work to the consolidated program benefits

6. Program stakeholder communications and management

Project Interaction

The interaction and information flow between the program and projects is iterative. Typically, information will flow from the program to its projects during the early stages and from projects to the program during later stages.

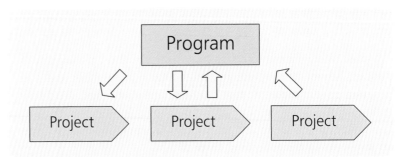

Program Management Characteristics

In the previous chapter we looked at some characteristics of project management. We can now use those same characteristics to define what is different about program management:

- **Change:** while project managers try to minimize change, due to the duration of programs, program managers not only expect change but actively encourage it in order to maximize the strategic benefits of the program

- **Leadership Style:** while project managers focus on getting team members to do work on the project, program managers focus on managing relationships, conflict resolution and the political aspects of stakeholder management

- **Management Skills:** while project managers focus on team motivation, program managers need to provide overall vision and leadership

- **Monitoring:** while project managers focus on task completion, program managers monitor the projects and program-related work through the program governance structure

- **People Management:** while project managers have no direct authority over their teams, program managers manage the project managers

- **Planning:** program managers are responsible for performing high level planning and providing guidance to project managers for their detailed project planning

- **Scope:** while a project has a narrow scope, a program has a wider scope and is dedicated to meeting the benefit goals of the organization. The scope of the program can also change to meet evolving goals

- **Success:** program success is measured in terms of return on investment (ROI), benefit realization and new operational capabilities delivered by the program

In summary, a program is designed to deliver benefits in line with strategic objectives. The program is executed through a number of projects. The program manager ensures that the projects will meet the objectives of the program and deliver the desired benefits.

Benefits Management

Benefits management is the second of the four management themes that are said to run through programs. These themes help to drive the program efforts towards the strategic objectives and benefits for which the program is designed. Although the overall management of the program is important, management of benefits and their realization is critical to the success of the program.

Benefits

A benefit is anything that makes a positive financial contribution or an improvement to the running of an organization. This could be increased revenue, reduced cost or even improved employee morale. And these benefits can be tangible or intangible:

- **Tangible Benefits:** are quantifiable benefits that can be directly related to the financial objectives such as a 10% increase in sales or a five percent reduction in costs

- **Intangible benefits:** are benefits that are not so easy to quantify such as improved employee morale or increased customer satisfaction. However, most intangible benefits eventually end up contributing to tangible benefits (increased customer satisfaction leads to increased sales)

Benefits Management

Benefits management consists of defining and formalizing the benefits that the program is expected to deliver. These are then planned, modeled and tracked throughout the program life cycle. The following diagram illustrates the benefits management process that runs through the program:

Benefits Management

| Benefits Identification | Benefits Analysis | Benefits Planning | Benefits Realization | Benefits Transition |

Programs are run in order to realize benefits to the business, so benefits management must begin right at the start of the program and run through until after the completion of the program.

Hot tip

Benefits are the main justification for running a project or a program.

The steps in the benefits management process are as follows:

1   **Benefits Identification:** expected benefits will usually be defined before being allocated to a program for realization; they need to be quantified and assessed to ensure they are realistic, specific, measurable and can be realized within a specified time period

2   **Benefits Analysis:** benefits then need to be mapped onto the component projects which will deliver them, metrics developed for how they will be measured and the individual projects examined to identify interdependencies of benefits between different projects

3   **Benefits Planning:** a benefits realization plan needs to be produced in the early stages of a program and maintained throughout the program. It should include a definition of each benefit and a description of how it will be realized (including roles and responsibilities for benefits management and delivery of the actual benefits) together with a benefits communications plan

4   **Benefits Realization:** as the component projects are implemented and the benefits start to accrue to the business, the actual benefits achieved need to be monitored and tracked against the benefits realization plan and program performance tracked and reported

5   **Benefits Transition:** at the conclusion of the program not all of the expected benefits will yet have been realized, so responsibilities need to be transitioned from the program to ongoing operations management for ongoing tracking and reporting of the benefits achieved

Change Management

Any time a program change is planned, it needs to be analyzed to determine its potential impact on the realization of benefits or benefits outcome. Any changes must be reflected back into the benefits realization plan and the impact communicated to all interested parties and key stakeholders.

Stakeholder Management

As with benefits management, stakeholder management has to start right at the outset of a program. It is important for the success of the program that these individuals or organizations are identified and that they are communicated with effectively throughout the life of the program.

Stakeholders

Program stakeholders are individuals and organizations whose interests may be affected (either positively or negatively) by the outcomes of a program. Stakeholders therefore fall into two categories: positive stakeholders (who will benefit from the program) and negative stakeholders (who see some disadvantage in the program). The implications are that the positive stakeholders will want to see the program succeed while the negative stakeholders will be happier to see the program abandoned. For example, building a new waste incinerator plant may make environmentalists happy, but it will not make people who live in the immediate vicinity of it happy at all.

Program stakeholder management extends beyond project stakeholder management. Program stakeholders can arise from dependencies among the projects and from the wholeness of the program (the consolidated benefits and capabilities). The following list is only a starting point: program and project managers, program and project office, program and project team members, customers and suppliers (internal or external), program sponsor or director and the governance board.

PESTLE

Another useful acronym for identifying potential stakeholders is to consider the: Political, Environmental, Sociological, Technological, Legal and Economic interests that might be impacted by or have an impact on the program.

Stakeholder Management

Clearly the first step in stakeholder management is to identify the key stakeholders:

 Identify Stakeholders: begin to identify stakeholders (both positive and negative) as early as possible in the program. Missing any stakeholders could have a damaging impact on the program, so try to identify them all

Negative stakeholders are often overlooked by program managers, which increases risks to the program.

46

Great care needs to be taken in dealing and communicating with negative stakeholder.

2   **Needs and Expectations:** having identified the stakeholders their needs and expectations have to be understood; different stakeholders may have very different and even conflicting expectations that should be understood and analyzed, so they can be managed

3   **Stakeholder Management Plan:** develop a stakeholder management plan based on the individual stakeholders' needs and expectations; this should identify their communication needs, the information they will want and how often they will need to be communicated with

4   **Communication Strategy:** develop a communication strategy covering how you will deliver consistent information to all stakeholders in a proactive, targeted and timely fashion. This will help to manage stakeholder expectations, develop a clear understanding of the issues and reduce the number of conflicts and misunderstandings that may occur

Beware

Underestimating stakeholder influence when identifying requirements can prove to be very costly later.

Change Management

In program management, the key focus should always be on the benefits the program will deliver. However, in any program some changes will probably be necessary. Therefore, it is important to identify the stakeholders who will be affected by any change and ensure that they are aware of and supportive of the change by making them part of the change process:

1   Communicate a clear vision of the need for and objectives of the change together with the resources required for it

2   Set clear goals, develop a plan for the change and agree it with the key stakeholders

3   Monitor the change as it is implemented and keep the key stakeholders in the picture

4   Obtain feedback from stakeholders who are affected by the change and address any issues they may have

Program Governance

Program governance should be viewed in the context of corporate governance, which refers to the practice of developing, implementing and monitoring the processes, policies, procedures and organizational structures needed to run an organization while following the laws of the land. It should also be viewed in the light of the organization's mission, vision and strategy:

Mission

The mission is a statement of the organization's goals and objectives, what it does and the reason for its existence; it is expressed in a mission statement, such as "To provide the best widgets and after sales service in the business".

Vision

The vision is a description of the desired future state of the organization. Unlike the mission statement (which is a statement of current objectives), the vision statement represents where the organization wants to be in the future, such as "To become the world's leading supplier of widgets".

Strategy

Strategy refers to the long-term plan of action designed to achieve the objectives as represented in the mission and vision statements.

Based on corporate governance together with the organization's mission, vision and strategy; program governance therefore addresses the development, communication, implementation and monitoring of policies, procedures, organization structure and other activities associated with a program. It is intended to provide:

1. A framework for efficient and effective decision making

2. Consistent delivery management with a focus on achieving program goals

3. An appropriate mechanism to address risks and stakeholder requirements

Program governance is normally implemented by a program board (or steering committee as it is sometimes known) assisted by a program office as illustrated in the following diagram:

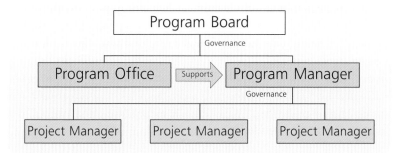

Program Board

The program board provides an executive forum, responsible for the governance and quality assurance of a program. It is typically a cross-functional group of senior stakeholders and exists for the life of the program. The functions of a program board include:

1. Approving the initial program plan and any subsequent changes to it

2. Ensuring the program is compliant with corporate and legal policies, procedures, requirements and standards

3. Ensuring the availability of adequate and suitable resources for the program

4. Guiding the program manager on any risks and issues

5. Establishing the framework and limits for decision making on investments in the program

6. Reviewing the program's progress, cost and benefits delivery

7. Approving the program moving to the next phase

Program governance is largely concerned with monitoring and controlling two factors: organization investment and benefits delivery. This is achieved by monitoring progress reports and reviews on a regular basis throughout the life of the program.

Program Life Cycle

From authorization to completion, a program goes through a life cycle (referred to as the transformational flow in MSP) that includes: defining the program objectives, planning the work to achieve those objectives, performing the work, monitoring the progress and closing the program. In the same way as a project is divided into stages for control, a program is more effectively managed and controlled by dividing it into phases. The phases of a program life cycle are shown in the following illustration:

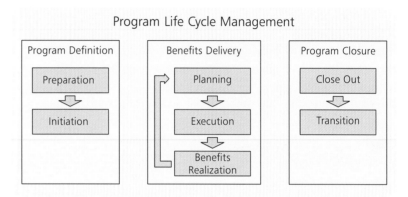

Program Life Cycle Management

Program Definition

The purpose of this phase is to establish a firm foundation of support and approval for the program. It consists of two stages:

1. **Preparation Stage:** builds on the outline program proposal by developing a high level business case, selecting a program manager, developing a high level plan for the program and a detailed plan for the initiation stage, obtaining the support of the key stakeholders and submitting the proposal to the appropriate authority for approval to proceed

2. **Initiation Stage:** following approval of the proposal, the program manager is appointed, the program infrastructure (including program facilities, program board and any tools) is put in place, key deliverables from the program are identified and a detailed plan for how they will be delivered is developed and costed. This is then agreed with all key stakeholders and submitted for approval to proceed to the next phase (benefits delivery)

Benefits Delivery

During this major phase, the constituent projects are initiated and inter-project activities are coordinated to deliver the benefits. There are three stages for each project:

1 **Planning:** each project needs to be planned by the project team and the plan approved by the program manager

2 **Execution:** once approved, the project is carried out by the project team under the governance of the program manager

3 **Benefits Realization:** once the project has been implemented successfully the benefits can be monitored and overall program performance against plan tracked

These three stages are completed for each component project. Once all the projects have been completed, the program can (with authorization) move onto the closure phase.

Program Closure

The purpose of this phase is to perform a controlled close down of the program. There are two stages to this:

1 **Close Out:** to document the results of the program, capture the lessons learned and shut down the program infrastructure

2 **Transition:** to hand over any program artifacts to the operational group responsible along with responsibility for ongoing benefits monitoring

Process Groups

The processes involved can be allocated to the same five process groups as for project management: Initiating (defining and authorizing the program and projects within the program); Planning (the program and constituent projects); Executing (using resources in an integrated fashion to deliver the benefits); Monitoring and Controlling (the program and the constituent projects); and Closing (the program and the constituent projects).

Program Controls

Program controls form part of program governance and are the mechanisms by which the program management processes are monitored. Controls can be any activities, policies, or procedures that are used to govern the execution of a process to ensure that the process works in a consistent and predictable fashion.

Program controls also feed into the process improvement (or experiential learning) cycle of: improve, implement, measure and review (as illustrated in the diagram on the right).

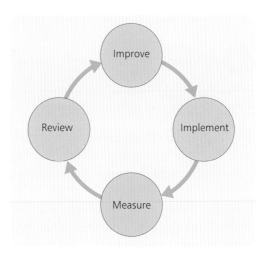

Some common examples of program controls are as follows:

Audits

These can be an evaluation of any process, project, program or product to verify its compliance with the standards and procedures defined by the organization. An audit might check if the information reported about the program is supported by actual data or whether the program is compliant with corporate quality, risk or financial standards.

Contracts

Any contracts entered into by a program or one of its component projects will have contract terms and conditions which have to be complied with, so contracts also act as controls.

Policies and Procedures

Organizations use policies and procedures to enforce the consistent implementation of processes, standards and work methods. An organization policy may require that certain sections must be present in the program management plan or it may specify a process for obtaining approval for a program document such as the program charter or program management plan. So corporate policies and procedures are also controls.

Program Plans

A program is driven by the objectives it must meet, so the program plans (which also contain these objectives) can also act as program controls. Program progress and performance are measured against the actual achievement of these business objectives as compared to the plan.

Reviews

Program reviews can be performed for a variety of purposes related to monitoring and controlling, such as: verifying compliance, identifying issues and assessing progress. Regular reviews are used as controls on many of the standard program management processes.

Standards

Standards may be developed by the organization itself through its program office or by industry groups or government bodies; in order to specify that things should be done in a standard way. These standards may be invoked in program documents (such as program plans) and will therefore control the program in that way.

Hot tip

Program office is covered on page 56.

53

Projects and Programs

A program is run to meet the business objectives, as set out in the strategic plan of an organization. Controls are used to control the processes, which in turn are used to run the program. Processes are also used to run the projects which are components of the program and these can likewise be controlled.

There is a logical relationship between the strategic plan, program and projects. The program is created to meet the strategic plan of the organization and the projects are created by the program. A program may also be formed to bring together several projects which can be grouped together into a program to achieve greater control and benefits. However, it does not change the functional relationship between the three entities: the projects are executed as part of the program and the program is executed to implement the strategic plan and objectives of the organization.

Process Improvement

As mentioned at the start of this topic, controls are one of the things that can feed into the process improvement cycle. To maximize the benefits, the results should be fed into the review and improve stages of the cycle via the program office.

Hot tip

Process improvement (via capability maturity) and program office are covered in the next two topics.

Capability Maturity

In Chapter 2 we looked at project management maturity and the capability maturity five level model. The model works in exactly the same way with program management maturity.

Program Management Maturity

The model provides a theoretical continuum along which process maturity can be developed incrementally from one level to the next, as illustrated in the diagram below:

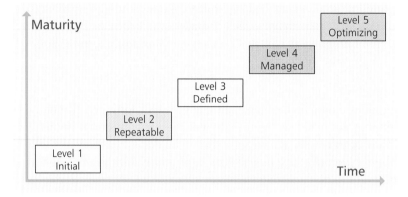

Each maturity level has its key process areas which characterize that level and these are the stages that organizations must go through to become mature (skipping levels is neither allowed nor feasible). The definition of the five levels is:

Level 1: Initial

Processes at this level are undocumented and in a state of dynamic change, driven in a reactive manner by events. The organization may or may not recognize programs and run them differently to projects. Programs are started without gathering all the business requirements. There are no scope, cost, quality, people, communication or risk standards or processes in place. No program office has been established.

Level 2: Repeatable

Some processes are now repeatable, possibly with consistent results. Process discipline is still unlikely to be rigorous, but where it exists it may help to ensure that the processes are maintained during times of stress. Each program is run with its own processes and procedures to a minimum standard. There will be a general statement of business requirements but little scope management.

No standard practices for budgeting, quality, resourcing or risk management will be in place. A project office may have been established but with no single point of responsibility.

Level 3: Defined
Defined and documented standard processes have been established and are subject to some degree of improvement over time. These standard processes are used to establish consistency across the organization. The organization has its own centrally controlled program processes and individual programs can flex within these to suit the particular program. Basic management processes have now been established and some scope management may now exist. Cost, time, quality, communication and risk management policies are in place but probably only followed on larger programs.

Level 4: Managed
Process capability is established and by using process metrics, management can effectively control the standard processes for program management. Management can identify ways to adjust and adapt the process to particular programs with no measurable loss of quality or deviations from specifications. Processes are fully documented and used by most programs. Stakeholders actively participate in scope decisions. Standards and processes are in place for cost, quality, people, communication and risk management. The project office is now well developed. The organization obtains specific measurements on its program management performance and runs a quality management organization to better predict future program outcomes.

Level 5: Optimizing
The focus now is on continually improving process performance through incremental and innovative changes and improvements. Processes are concerned with addressing common causes of process variation and changing the process to improve process performance. This would be done at the same time as maintaining the likelihood of achieving the established quantitative process-improvement objectives. Programs are now managed and evaluated in the light of other programs. Historical data is used to forecast future performance and standard processes are now used across all the knowledge areas. The program office is now managing all processes and organizational standards.

The role of the program office is covered in the next topic.

Program Office

Program office (sometimes called a program management office or program support office) is a vital part of the capability maturity process. It is a central support group, designed to provide guidance and assistance to programs throughout the organization.

Program Office Role

A program office might initially be set up to provide support to a single program or it could have a wider remit to provide support to programs and projects across the organization. Typically, the program office is responsible for defining and managing program-related governance procedures, processes, documentation standards and templates for all the programs in the organization.

Training and Support

The program office should be the centre of excellence for the organization, providing program and project management training and support. It can provide support to project managers in the day-to-day running of their projects and assist in the application of techniques to keep projects on time and within budget. The program office can handle the program administration functions by providing support to each program management team.

Methodologies

It develops and maintains the methodologies used by the organization and adopts recommendations from previous lessons learned. It improves communication by having common processes, deliverables and terminology.

Document Library

It sets up and supports a common document library so that prior program and project management deliverables can be candidates for reuse by similar projects. The program office should establish and implement a common set of reusable processes and templates to save time and effort on program and project start up.

Metrics and Reporting

It will track organization-wide metrics on the state of project and program delivery and provide reports and feedback to senior management on this.

It can also provide an early warning system that can indicate where future problems may arise and reduce any repetition of problems previously experienced.

Program Assurance

The program office is also the centre for governance and control, including program assurance, standards, approvals, financial monitoring and the provision of health checks. Assurance is carried out in order to generate confidence that a program is being managed effectively and that it is on track to realize the expected benefits and achieve the desired outcomes.

Implementation

Setting up a program office is a fairly straightforward process involving the following:

1 If a project office has not been established, then set this up first (using the process on page 35)

2 Obtain executive approval for the establishment and support of a program office

3 Define the organization's program management methods, procedures, standards and guidelines (with the involvement of any existing program and project managers) and obtain executive approval for these

4 Appoint one or more staff as necessary to run the program office functions (ideally including staff who already have experience of the project office)

5 Provide any training required for the project office staff in the new functions to enable them to carry out their roles

6 Provide any training required by program managers in the use of the program office documentation and functions

7 Set up regular process reviews between the program office and the program managers, to ensure the development and improvement of standards and methods

Once established, the program office will be able to collect and hand over lessons learned from one program to the next.

A set of checklists for implementing project, program and portfolio office is available on our website. Go to **www.ineasysteps. com/resource-centre/ downloads/**

57

The program office will need to have processes that are tightly integrated with the finance department for budgeting, forecasting and monitoring project and program spend.

Summary

- A program is a dossier of related projects managed in a coordinated way to deliver benefits and control not available by managing each project individually

- Program management is the coordinated management of a program in order to achieve its goals, strategic objectives and benefits

- There are said to be three other management themes that run through a program: stakeholder management, benefits management and program governance

- Program management deals with things outside of the remit of project managers such as: inter-project dependencies, prioritization between projects and tracking the contribution of each project to the strategic goals and objectives of the organization

- Benefits are anything that makes a positive financial contribution or improvement to the organization

- Benefits management consists of defining the benefits the program is expected to deliver, planning for and tracking the realization of them through the program life cycle

- Stakeholders are individuals and organizations whose interests may be affected (positively or negatively) by the outcomes of a program

- Stakeholder management involves the identification of stakeholders and the management of their expectations and communications needs

- Program governance is related to corporate governance and involves development, implementation and monitoring of the processes, policies, procedures and organizational structures needed to run the program

- The program life cycle consists of three phases: program definition, benefits delivery (planning, execution and benefits realization for each project) and program closure

- Program office is a central support group providing support, guidance, compliance and quality assurance to programs

4 Portfolio Management

This chapter explains what portfolio management means and involves, together with the implications of introducing it into an organization.

Portfolio

The word portfolio was originally used to describe a type of briefcase, typically containing a collection of papers. The term was then extended to cover an artist's portfolio, a somewhat larger object, containing samples of an artist's work. In government, the term portfolio is used to describe the post and responsibilities of a head of a government department (ministry).

More recently, it was used to describe a financial portfolio, or collection of assets held by an institution or a private individual and, in the world of project management, the term was chosen to describe the entire collection of projects in an organization.

Project Portfolio

The project portfolio (or just portfolio) in our context is the term used to describe the total set of programs, stand-alone projects and other change initiatives being undertaken by an organization.

In the same way that a portfolio of investments is the totality of an individual's or organization's investments, a portfolio of programs and projects represents the totality of the organization's programs and projects. The reason for creating a portfolio is to provide an overall business view and control over all these programs and projects at a high level in the organization.

Portfolio management is sometimes referred to as 'enterprise project management' and the goal is to ensure that the portfolio delivers in line with the business strategy of the enterprise.

Business Strategy

Business strategy can be defined as the chosen courses of action, together with the allocated resources, required to achieve the organization's objectives and gain competitive advantage.

Given that any organization has finite resources (both financial and human) there will clearly need to be some form of trade off between the conflicting demands for those resources. Portfolio management is the process of managing that trade off and the subsequent implementation and achievement of the expected business benefits.

We saw in the previous chapter that the main rationale for program management was either to deal with a number of related and interdependent projects or to break down one very large project into more manageable but consequentially related and interdependent projects. Portfolio management on the other hand, is concerned with the high-level management of all the organization's projects.

From this we can see that portfolio management can be implemented and practiced, whether or not an organization has implemented program management. Conversely, an organization can implement program management without implementing portfolio management. The two are different and complementary.

The following diagram illustrates the relationship between the organization's business strategy, its portfolio and its projects:

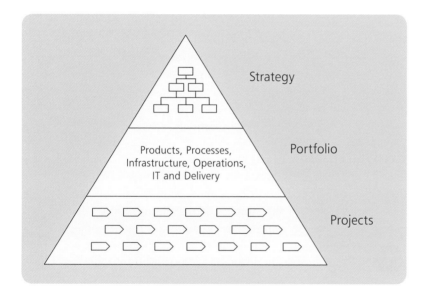

The strategy layer represents the organization's vision (what it wants to be like in future) at the top of the pyramid. This drives the mission (what it is aiming to achieve to meet that vision) and from that the strategy and objectives (what it is going to have to do in order to get there).

The portfolio layer represents the sum total of all the projects, supporting processes, infrastructure, operations and delivery that will be needed to achieve the strategy and objectives.

The projects layer represents the individual projects (and programs if program management is also being used) that will be executed to implement the strategy and objectives.

Hot tip

Organizations of any size can benefit from portfolio management and the smaller the organization the less time it should require.

Portfolio Management

Portfolio Management is defined as the centralized management of processes, methods and technologies to collectively manage a group of current and proposed projects. The objectives are to determine the optimal resource mix and schedule to best achieve the organization's operational and financial goals.

It is therefore concerned with making sure the organization makes the right investments and gets the returns it needs (benefits) for organizational growth and the delivery of its mission. This means deciding which programs and projects to run and which not to.

Why Portfolio Management?

Without this additional layer of management, programs and projects may end up being authorized for all the wrong reasons. Business units may decide they can afford to run a 'nice to have' program or project as they have some funds available. But viewed from the organizational level there may be far more strategically important requirements that could better use the resources. With portfolio management, programs and projects are selected based on what they contribute to corporate objectives.

Key Objectives

All projects should be based on a viable business case and their inclusion in the portfolio should be justified in terms of their alignment with the strategy of the organization. Portfolio management can be summarized as having three key objectives:

1. To maximize the value of the portfolio by achieving the best possible return on investment

2. To align the portfolio with the organizational strategy by selecting projects that meet the needs of the business

3. To balance the portfolio by making the best possible use of the organization's human and financial resources

Business Strategy

Clearly, a prerequisite for portfolio management is that the business strategy and objectives have been defined. The business strategy is then represented as a portfolio (collection) of programs, projects and supporting operations.

Portfolio Management Characteristics

In the previous two chapters we looked at the characteristics of project and program management. We can now look at how portfolio management compares with these:

- **Change:** portfolio managers continuously monitor change both within the organization and in the business environment

- **Leadership Style:** focused on relationship management and achieving organizational agreement on strategy

- **Management Skills:** provide strategic vision and leadership to programs and projects

- **Monitoring:** portfolio managers monitor strategic change, resource allocation, portfolio performance and risk

- **People Management:** portfolio managers may manage or coordinate the portfolio office, program and project managers

- **Planning:** portfolio managers focus on the planning processes and communication requirements of the portfolio

- **Scope:** portfolios have an organizational scope that will change in line with the objectives of the organization

- **Success:** is measured in terms of the overall performance, benefits realization and use of resources of the portfolio

Management Skills

The Gartner Group (the world's leading information technology research and advisory company) identified portfolio management as an area that currently has a low level of definition and organizational maturity in all areas of industry. Yet, conversely, it is an area that carries a high level of risk and requires a high level of executive attention.

Introducing change by authorizing and then carrying out a large portfolio of projects is a complex undertaking requiring creativity, management skills, leadership, flexibility, the ability to accept setbacks calmly and the willingness to accept risks.

Later in this chapter we will look at two portfolio management methodologies which define some of the detailed skills required.

Hot tip

Chapter 9: Managing a Portfolio runs through the role of the portfolio manager in detail.

Portfolio Selection

The portfolio represents all of the approved projects that will be carried out under the sponsorship of senior management in the organization. These projects will be competing for scarce resources (financial and human) as there will rarely be sufficient resources to carry out every proposed project. Portfolio selection is the process that needs to be carried out from time to time, based on proposed projects and projects that are currently in progress.

Selecting the Portfolio

It may well be that a newly proposed project is more critical to the organization than one that is already part-completed. Portfolio selection therefore requires decisions to be made in line with the business strategy of the organization.

The ideal candidates are high value projects that are aligned to the business strategy. But the right number and balance of projects need to be selected to achieve the objectives. The best organizations tend to follow a formal method of portfolio selection and management:

Hot tip

Some organizations have a cut-off point, where low cost projects can be run by departments but larger projects must be submitted to portfolio selection.

1 Prioritize the right projects by involving key decision makers in the prioritization, planning and control

2 Establish the viability of projects based on their strategic alignment, return on investment and resource requirement

3 Carry out risk assessment and build contingency into the portfolio by integrating contingency planning

4 Do more with less by systematically reviewing project management processes and removing inefficiencies

5 Ensure informed decisions and governance by bringing together all project collaborators and processes

6 Extend best practice by continually vetting project management processes and capturing best practices

7 Understand future resource needs by aligning the right resources to the right projects at the right time

Portfolio Optimization

Once the potential projects have been selected, the decision has to be made about which projects to fund. The process is compounded by changing information, dynamic opportunities, multiple goals, interdependence between projects and multiple decision makers. Portfolio optimization is the process of formally making the best decisions possible under these conditions.

1 The first step in considering a project for inclusion is a preliminary assessment of its potential contribution to the business; whether it will meet a strategic objective or only an operational requirement

2 The second step is to consider the effort required to carry it out in terms of human resources, financial resources (cost/benefit) and associated risks

3 The projects can then be optimized using something like a MuSCoW (Must Have, Should Have, Could Have, Won't Have) grid, as illustrated below:

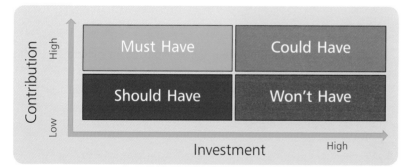

Hot tip

If an operational (low contribution) project is a prerequisite for a 'must have' strategic project, it should be treated as a strategic project itself.

Projects that provide the greatest return (contribution) on investment (cost and people) in line with the organization's strategy and risk tolerance are "must have" projects. Projects that provide a lower return but do not require a high investment are "should have" projects. Projects that promise a high contribution but will also require a substantial investment are only "could have" projects (as the resources are probably better used somewhere else). High cost and low contribution projects are not worth the investment and therefore "won't have" projects.

Standard for Portfolio Management

One of the two most widely used portfolio management methodologies (the other is covered in the next topic), the PMI's Standard for Portfolio Management (SPM) sets out to identify the portfolio management practices (knowledge, processes, skills, tools and techniques) that are recognized as best practice.

It defines a portfolio as a collection of component projects, programs and operations, managed as a group to achieve strategic objectives. The components must be quantifiable so they can be ranked and prioritized.

Portfolio Management

SPM defines the processes used to evaluate, select, prioritize and allocate resources to components that best accomplish the organizational strategy and objectives. Portfolio management focuses on doing the right work rather than doing the work right (which is the role of the project managers).

Portfolio managers consolidate information on the component performance to provide information to the portfolio management governing body on how the portfolio components are performing, together with recommendations for any required actions.

The standard assumes that the organization has in place strategy, objectives, mission and vision statements, together with goals, objectives and strategies to achieve the vision. The goal is then to establish a balanced portfolio that will help the organization achieve its goals by:

1. Aligning the portfolio to the organization's strategic objectives

2. Allocating human, financial, material or equipment resources to enable components to be executed

3. Measuring the performance of individual components (programs and projects) in the context of its goals

4. Managing risks to the portfolio and its components

The standard defines three portfolio management process groups and five knowledge areas.

Process Groups

The three process groups are:

1 **Defining:** how the strategic objectives will be implemented and the portfolio authorized, together with the development of the portfolio management plan

2 **Aligning:** determine how the portfolio will be aligned to the organization's strategic plan by optimizing, determining value and developing risk responses

3 **Authorizing and Controlling:** define how changes will be monitored, track and review performance indicators, authorize the portfolio and verify the values obtained

Knowledge Areas

It also defines five knowledge (portfolio management skills) areas:

1 **Strategic Management:** to align the portfolio to strategic objectives by validating the strategic plan and defining the portfolio structure and road map

2 **Governance Management:** to develop the portfolio management plan and define, optimize and authorize the portfolio

3 **Performance Management:** to develop the performance management plan (including financial management) and balancing the supply and demand of resource

4 **Communication Management:** to ensure the timely and appropriate generation, collection, distribution, storage and retrieval of portfolio information

5 **Risk Management:** planning, risk identification, risk analysis, response planning, and monitoring and controlling the portfolio

Management of Portfolios

The other popular methodology is the OGC's Management of Portfolios (MoP). This methodology defines a portfolio as the totality of an organization's investment in the changes required to achieve its strategic objectives. It defines portfolio management as a coordinated collection of strategic processes and decisions that together enable the most effective balance of organizational change and ongoing operational management.

They claim it will result in more of the right programs and projects being undertaken, more effectively and with greater benefits realization. They state that the methodology will be most successful where there is an established culture of program and project management in place, but also say that this is not a prerequisite for its successful implementation (see warning left).

The methodology consists of five principles, two management cycles and twelve portfolio management practices. Unlike SPM, the method makes no distinction about when the principles, cycles and practices should be used. In fact it states that they are all used at the same time but with varying degrees of intensity, depending on the organization and the environment in which it is working.

Principles

The five principles represent the foundations upon which effective portfolio management is built:

1 Senior management commitment and support

2 Governance alignment to existing corporate governance and decision making

3 Strategy alignment with the organization's strategic objectives

4 A functioning portfolio office

5 An energized change culture in the organization

Portfolio management practices take place within two continuous cycles: the definition cycle and delivery cycle, with their supporting management practices:

Beware

Warning: Implementing portfolio management without an established culture of project management in place is not recommended.

Portfolio Definition Cycle

Doing the right things through the following:

1 Understand the scope of the portfolio

2 Categorize components based on their alignment to the strategic objectives

3 Prioritize the change initiatives within the portfolio by ranking them

4 Balance the portfolio based on timing, contribution, impact, risk and resource requirement and availability

5 Produce the portfolio strategy and delivery plan

Portfolio Delivery Cycle

Doing those things right through the following:

1 Management control of the delivery of the component programs and projects

2 Management of benefits through benefits planning and realization

3 Financial management of the portfolio

4 Risk management of the portfolio and components

5 Stakeholder engagement, communication and management

6 Organizational governance of the portfolio

7 Resource management across the portfolio

Either of these standards and methodologies would form a good starting point for the implementation of portfolio management.

Hot tip

The next topic sets out a generic approach that is applicable to but does not depend on either methodology.

Portfolio Life Cycle

Portfolio management, once introduced in an organization, should be an ongoing process. The portfolio will typically span several years, but it will be subject to ongoing change. In portfolio management change is not bad, it is expected and regarded as a positive aspect. Over time, the business environment in which an organization operates will change and evolve, often quite rapidly.

To be successful an organization needs to change and evolve in line with the environment and also to take advantage of new opportunities. This means the vision, mission and strategy will change and therefore the portfolio must change to reflect that by re-examining all existing programs, projects and operations and any new potential programs, projects or operations.

Both the methodologies examined define an ongoing or cyclical process, one with two management cycles (portfolio definition and portfolio delivery), the other with three process groups (defining, aligning, and authorizing and controlling).

As the defining and aligning process groups map onto the portfolio definition cycle, and the authorizing and controlling process group maps onto the portfolio delivery management cycle, there is no conflict between the methodologies at this level. The following illustration therefore summarizes the portfolio life cycle in a way that is independent of but compatible with either of these methodologies:

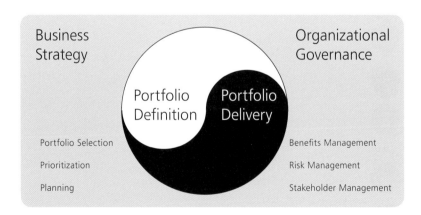

The ancient yin and yang symbol epitomizes the cyclical nature of the portfolio life cycle and the interdependence of the portfolio definition and portfolio delivery phases.

The two drivers for the portfolio life cycle are the business strategy and the organizational governance:

Business Strategy

The business strategy, based on the organization's vision and mission statements, drives the portfolio definition phase:

1   **Portfolio Selection:** based on an understanding of the scope of the portfolio together with existing change initiatives and new requirements

2   **Portfolio Prioritization:** the change initiatives in the portfolio are ranked based on the agreed metrics, then balanced based on timing, contribution to strategic objectives, business impact, risk and available resources

3   **Portfolio Plan:** the information is then collated to create the portfolio strategy and delivery plan for authorization

Organizational Governance

Organizational governance is based on the portfolio manager and the portfolio board (or steering group) providing management control of the portfolio delivery:

1   **Benefits Management:** identification and management of the benefits being realized from the portfolio and the contribution it makes to operational performance and strategic objectives

2   **Risk Management:** the consistent and effective management of the portfolio's exposure to risk at the individual project and portfolio level

3   **Stakeholder Management:** identification and management of the needs of the portfolio's stakeholders, together with the resource management to deliver the changes

This generic portfolio life cycle has been developed to work with either of the two identified methodologies or it can be used as the basis for defining an organization's own procedures.

Capability Maturity

In Chapters 2 and 3 we looked at project and program management maturity using the five level model. The model works in exactly the same way with portfolio management maturity.

Portfolio Management Maturity

Each maturity level again has its key process areas which characterize that level together with the goals, commitment, ability, measurement and verification. The following diagram illustrates the five stages of portfolio management maturity that an organization must go through to be fully mature:

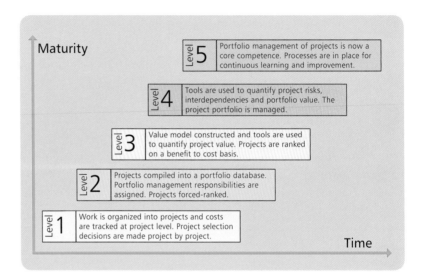

Maturity

Level **5** Portfolio management of projects is now a core competence. Processes are in place for continuous learning and improvement.

Level **4** Tools are used to quantify project risks, interdependencies and portfolio value. The project portfolio is managed.

Level **3** Value model constructed and tools are used to quantify project value. Projects are ranked on a benefit to cost basis.

Level **2** Projects compiled into a portfolio database. Portfolio management responsibilities are assigned. Projects forced-ranked.

Level **1** Work is organized into projects and costs are tracked at project level. Project selection decisions are made project by project.

Time

As with the project and program models, the portfolio model provides a theoretical continuum along which capability maturity can be developed incrementally from levels one to five. Once again, skipping levels is neither feasible nor achievable.

Level 1: Initial

Portfolio management processes at this level are typically undocumented and in a fairly chaotic state. The organization may or may not even understand what a portfolio is. There is no portfolio office in place and there is a complete lack of any portfolio management.

There may be an awareness of program management and one or more programs may have even been started but projects are still selected on a project-by-project evaluation basis and project progress, costs and resource usage is just tracked at the project (or program if they are part of a program) level.

Level 2: Repeatable

There is now some awareness and understanding of portfolio management and some processes have been documented and are repeatable (possibly with consistent results). The best collection of projects to be carried out with the resources available is identified and the projects are selected on that basis. This requires that project data is recorded in a central database, projects are ranked and portfolio management responsibilities are assigned.

Level 3: Defined

Defined and documented portfolio management processes have now been established and are subject to some degree of improvement over time. Metrics, models and tools for estimating the value of projects on a benefits-to-cost basis are in place and are always used.

Projects are now ranked on a return on investment basis and the portfolio is maximized on the basis of value for money. However, project interdependencies may be ignored.

Level 4: Managed

Portfolio management process capability has now been established and can be adapted to the needs of the portfolio with no loss of quality. Standards and processes are in place and are followed. Key stakeholders are fully involved in the decision making processes.

Improved tools and metrics now allow for project risk and interdependencies to be included in the evaluation process. The portfolio office is now well developed. Portfolio management is getting close to being optimized.

Level 5: Optimizing

The focus in now on continuous improvement to the portfolio management processes. Processes are in place for continuous learning and improvement and portfolio performance is now evaluated in the light of previous performance.

Portfolio management is now a core competence in the organization and the portfolio office is now managing all processes and organizational standards.

Hot tip

Establishing a portfolio office is covered in the next topic.

Portfolio Office

A portfolio office (or portfolio management office as it is sometimes called), is a central support group, designed to provide guidance and assistance to the organization's portfolio manager. The majority of organizations will only have one portfolio and portfolio manager, but in large organizations there may be more. In either case the portfolio office provides the same service.

The portfolio office should sit above the programs and projects, and provide an independent view of all change initiatives within the organization.

Portfolio Office Role

The role of the portfolio office starts at the project level:

1 Ensure that each project's business case is commercially realistic and has an honest examination of the risks to project delivery and benefits realization

2 Once this has been established: prioritize the projects put forward for funding by comparing costs, benefits, risks and strategic alignment of the candidate projects; then select the subset of the projects that on balance offer the highest benefit with the lowest cost and risk, within the organization's available cost and resource budgets (to create the candidate project portfolio)

3 Once the portfolio is approved and projects start to be implemented, the portfolio office should track: benefits realization, resource management, strategic risk and issue management, strategic planning and corporate finance and governance as it applies to the portfolio

4 Provide administrative support to the portfolio manager and portfolio management team and assurance to the organization about the management of the portfolio

5 The portfolio office is also responsible for defining and managing the governance procedures, processes and templates used in portfolio management and should aim to become the center of excellence for portfolio management in the organization

Hot tip

In a smaller organization the portfolio office role can sometimes be combined with that of the portfolio manager.

Implementation

Setting up a portfolio office is a fairly straightforward process involving the following:

1 If a project or program office has not yet been established, then set up a project office (see page 35) and also a program office (see page 57) if relevant

2 Obtain top management approval and commitment for the establishment and support of a portfolio office

3 Define the organization's portfolio management methods, procedures, standards and guidelines with the involvement of the portfolio manager (if appointed) and program and project managers. Obtain top management approval and support for these methods and procedures

4 Appoint the necessary staff (ideally including staff who already have experience in the program or project office) to carry out the portfolio office functions

5 Provide training for the portfolio office staff in the new processes and procedures as they are developed and introduced into the organization

6 Provide any training required for the portfolio, program and project managers in the functions of the portfolio office and their involvement with it

7 Set up regular process reviews between the portfolio office, portfolio manager and the program and project managers to ensure the development and improvement of portfolio methods and processes

Once established, the portfolio office can help to construct the optimal project portfolio, improve control over project justification and prioritization, value based prioritization of the portfolio and improve the probability of benefits realization. It can also develop and improve the portfolio management processes used.

Hot tip

A set of checklists for implementing project, program and portfolio office is available on our website. Go to www.ineasysteps. com/resource centre/ downloads/

Summary

- Portfolio is the term used to describe an organization's total set of programs, projects and other change initiatives

- The portfolio should be driven by the organization's strategy (vision, mission and objectives)

- Portfolio management is concerned with making sure the organization makes the right investment decisions and gets the returns (benefits) it needs to meet its strategy

- Portfolio selection is the process of reviewing the current and proposed projects and selecting the ones that most closely meet the requirements of the business

- Portfolio optimization refers to the final decision about which of the projects to fund with the available resources

- The first step in considering a project for inclusion in the portfolio is to establish its viability based on its potential value to the business

- The Standard for Portfolio Management (SPM) defines the portfolio management process through three process groups (defining, aligning, and authorizing and controlling) supported by five knowledge areas

- The Management of Portfolios (MoP) defines a methodology for portfolio management through two process groups (defining and delivery) supported by 12 knowledge areas

- A generic portfolio life cycle with the twin drivers of the business strategy and organizational governance will work with either of these methodologies

- As with project and program management, the capability maturity model works in exactly the same manner for portfolio management

- A key factor in establishing portfolio management maturity is the creation of a portfolio office

- The portfolio office is a central support group that provides guidance and assistance to the portfolio managers together with maintaining organizational standards

5 Organizational Maturity

This chapter explores organizational maturity in more depth. It looks at some related maturity models and introduces a plan for implementing organizational maturity.

Background

In the previous three chapters we explored project, program and portfolio management and an approach to measuring an organization's maturity in these processes. In order to achieve success in program or portfolio management and reach at least level three (defined), an organization will need to implement the supporting processes and achieve a degree of maturity in them.

Benefits

There are many good reasons for developing project, program and portfolio management (P3M) maturity, in particular these two:

- Organizations with a high level of maturity have a much lower project failure rate than organizations with a low level of maturity (around 50% better on average)

- Organizations with a low level of maturity typically find that the cost of project management represents around 11% of the total cost of projects; organizations that have established maturity find that the cost of managing projects is only around 6% (nearly half the cost)

So reducing the risk of project failure and reducing the cost of project management are pretty good starting points. Developing P3M maturity will also enable organizations to be better able to respond to the ever changing business environment through more effective projects.

Companies need the organizational capability to choose the right projects, manage costs and innovate. They need the organizational capability to deliver projects successfully, consistently and predictably. That all comes through organizational maturity.

Recent surveys both in the USA and UK found that the current state of the art with regard to project, program and portfolio management was as follows:

 In the majority of the organizations surveyed, project management was a well understood and well practiced discipline. Most of the organizations allow some flexibility in the methods being used for different sized projects (tailoring of methods to suit the project). Most of the organizations were at least at level two (repeatable) for project management maturity

2 Program management as a concept was also quite well understood in the majority of organizations; however very few of them were practicing it (with the exception of a handful of very large or complex projects). The majority of organizations are still on level one (initial) for program management maturity

3 The disturbing finding was that the concept of portfolio management was not understood at all in the majority of organizations. Most organizations are still on level one (initial) for portfolio management maturity

There is clearly the scope for any organization to gain competitive advantage by increasing their awareness of and developing their capability maturity in program and portfolio management.

Establishing P3M Maturity

Over the past few years there have been a number of initiatives to try to combine project management, program management and portfolio management maturity and two of these are explored, at a summary level, in the next topic (page 80). While these two methodologies are sound, they are not essential to establishing organizational maturity, and a step-by-step guide is included under Establishing Maturity (page 84).

Developing P3M Maturity

Having established the organization's current level of maturity, the next stage is to draw up a plan to move the organization up the maturity model levels. This is set out in easy steps from level one to level five (pages 86 to 93).

P3 Office

A key element in achieving maturity is the establishment of a supporting project, program and portfolio office. A model for this (P3O) has also been developed by the OGC and again, although the model is a sound one, it is not essential to setting up a project, program and portfolio office, as the steps to do this have also been included (page 94).

The remainder of this chapter will guide you through the process of establishing and developing organizational P3M maturity.

Maturity Models

Two project, program and portfolio management maturity models have emerged, both based on the capability maturity model. They are OPM3 from the PMI (covered below and opposite) and P3M3 from the OGC (starting on page 82).

OPM3

PMI states that its organizational project management maturity model (OPM3) is a best practice standard for assessing and developing an organization's capabilities in project, program and portfolio management. While it has retained the five CMM maturity levels, it has also (confusingly) changed their names:

Level 1: Ad Hoc
No formal standards, processes, methods or procedures exist and there are no staff to constitute a project management discipline. Standard technologies and reporting are sporadic.

Level 2: Planned
Project management standards, processes, methods, procedures, and staff exist in the organization but are not considered to be an organizational standard. Basic documentation exists but is inconsistent and there is little management support.

Level 3: Managed
All project management standards, processes, methods, procedures and staff are in place as organizational standards. Formal documentation exists along with consistent management support but execution is inconsistently applied.

Level 4: Integrated
More refined project management standards, processes, methods, procedures, documentation and staff are in place. Consistent management support is provided. Consistent execution and efficiency exist across all projects. There are metrics in place to collect performance data from all projects.

Level 5: Sustained
Lessons learned and best practices are applied to continuously improve existing standards, processes, methods, procedures, documentation and staff. Metrics are collected and applied at the project, portfolio and organizational levels. The organization is in a position to evaluate future decisions based on past performance and maximize its competitive advantage in the industry.

Measuring Maturity

OPM3 identifies 17 organizational enablers (areas where maturity can be measured). These cover areas such as: project success criteria, project management training, organizational project management methodology, strategic alignment, project management metrics and individual performance appraisals.

The process is based around three interlocking elements: knowledge (project management best practices), assessment (to establish the current level) and improvement (plan for and implement the required development). They say it should be implemented using the following steps (built around these three interlocking elements):

1. Plan and prepare for the assessment

2. Carry out the assessment using consultants or the self-assessment questionnaire (see note below)

3. Once the maturity level has been determined, develop a plan for improvements to the next level of maturity, based on the findings

4. Implement the improvements to take the organization to the next level through training and development

5. Repeat the process

Note: PMI recommends that the assessments are carried out by a professional consultant, but it does also supply a quite lengthy self-assessment questionnaire.

Based on the findings of the assessment, an improvement plan should be developed to reflect the organization's vision for enterprise project management. This should include the actions required to accomplish it over a suitable time frame.

OPM3 emphasizes that success comes from selecting the right projects in alignment with organizational strategies and implementing the processes, structures and behaviors necessary to deliver projects successfully, consistently and predictably.

...cont'd

P3M3

The OGC's project, program and portfolio management maturity model (P3M3) is developed from the capability maturity model and like OPM3 it uses the five standard maturity levels. Helpfully (unlike OPM3), it does not change their names:

Level 1: Initial

At this level processes are not usually documented and there are no or very few process descriptions.

Level 2: Repeatable

Basic management practices have now been established to track project expenditure and scheduling. Resources and processes are now being developed.

Level 3: Defined

The management and technical processes necessary to achieve the organizational purpose are now documented, standardized and integrated to some extent with other business processes.

Level 4: Managed

Mature behavior and processes are now quantitatively managed and controlled using metrics and quantitative techniques.

Level 5: Optimizing

The organization now focuses on optimization of its quantitatively managed processes to take into account changing business needs and external factors.

Measuring Maturity

In a slightly more straightforward approach than OPM3, P3M3 defines seven perspectives over which an organization is evaluated:

1. **Management Control:** of the change initiative and how its direction of travel is maintained throughout its life cycle, with appropriate break points to enable it to be stopped or redirected by a controlling body if necessary

2. **Benefits Management:** the process that ensures that the desired business change outcomes have been clearly defined, are measurable and are ultimately realized through a structured approach and with full organizational ownership

3   **Financial Management:** ensures that the likely costs of the initiative are captured and evaluated (within a formal business case) and that costs are categorized and managed over the investment life cycle

4   **Stakeholder Engagement:** is an ongoing process across all initiatives and one that is inherently linked to the initiative's life cycle and governance controls

5   **Risk Management:** defines the way in which the organization manages threats to, and opportunities presented by, the initiative

6   **Organizational Governance:** determines how the delivery of initiatives is aligned to the strategic direction of the organization. It considers how start up and closure controls are applied to initiatives and how alignment is maintained during an initiative's life cycle. This differs from management control, which views how control of initiatives is maintained internally

7   **Resource Management:** including human resources, buildings, equipment, supplies, information, tools and supporting teams. A key element of resource management is the process for acquiring resources and how supply chains are utilized to maximize effective use of resources

Both the OPM3 and P3M3 models can provide a structured approach to establishing and developing organizational project, program and portfolio management maturity. Either method could assist an organization in evaluating its current level and planning for its future development, but neither are essential as the process is a fairly straightforward one.

The remaining topics in this chapter provide the necessary steps for establishing an organization's current level of maturity, then planning for each step of the improvement process. Finally, as organizational maturity is dependent on the establishment of a project, program and portfolio office, it sets out the steps required to set one up.

Beware

Either of these methodologies could be over the top for a smaller organization. The rest of this chapter sets out a simple approach to developing maturity.

Establishing Maturity

The basic definitions of organizational maturity in project, program and portfolio management were set out towards the end of each of the previous three chapters.

Rate your Organizational Maturity

Using the models of project, program and portfolio management maturity as a starting point, the steps to establishing your organization's level of maturity are:

1 Establish the level of project management maturity (using the level descriptions on page 33) and select the level that most accurately describes your organization's current level of project management maturity

2 Now, repeat the process for program management maturity (using the level descriptions on pages 54 and 55) and again select the level that most accurately describes your organization's current level of maturity

3 Repeat the process a third time for portfolio management (using the level descriptions on pages 72 and 73) and again select the level that most accurately describes your organization's current level of maturity

Step two or three can be skipped if you are not planning to implement both program and portfolio management, but it is probably worth carrying out the exercise for completeness.

Assess the Results

Most organizations that are considering implementing program or portfolio management are likely to be at around level three for project management. They are also likely to be at level one for program and portfolio management.

If you rated your organization higher than this then your organization is in a good state to move onto program and portfolio management. Skip on to the next topic (page 86).

If you rated your organization at level three or below for project management, then this needs to be addressed before starting to implement program or portfolio management. Start at the appropriate place on the page opposite.

Level 1: Initial

If the organization is still at the initial state, then begin here and follow through the rest of the steps on this page:

1 Begin the process of documenting project management standards and methodologies or adopt one of the standard methodologies and define a suitable project life cycle (both covered in Chapter 2)

2 Involve the existing project managers in the organization in the process of selecting and documenting standards

Level 2: Repeatable

If the organization is at the repeatable state, then begin here and follow through the rest of the steps on this page:

3 Establish a project office (this only needs to be one person to start with) to maintain the documentation and interface with the project managers

4 Get management authorization (if needed) to enforce compliance with the established standards and monitor this through the project office

5 Involve the organization's project managers in reviewing and improving the standards

Level 3: Defined

If the organization is at the defined state, then begin here:

6 Task the project office with introducing process metrics for all project management standards and defining the amount of flexibility in the standards

7 Involve the organization's project managers in reviewing and improving the processes used for managing standards

The following five topics work through the project, program and portfolio management maturity levels, with the activities necessary to move up to the next level.

Beware

If the organization is still at level three: defined, don't be tempted to skip these steps.

A set of checklists for implementing P3 maturity levels one to five is available on our website. Go to **www.ineasysteps. com/resource-centre/ downloads/**

Level 1: Initial

Level 1 is the lowest level in the combined project, program and portfolio management model. However, it does assume that two key process areas are in place: project definition (level three) and program management awareness (level one).

Project Definition

The project definition process area assumes a common and agreed understanding within an organization that carries out projects, and that these projects are explicitly recognized. Confirm this by carrying out the following steps:

1. Every project should have documented objectives (which have been agreed by management) and adequate resources allocated to carry out the project

2. Every project should be managed by a project manager, performing basic project management activities such as planning and organizing the work of the project

3. Every project should have a defined project life cycle and outline project plan (based on stages or phases) evidencing high level planning

4. Any changes to project objectives or requirements (scope) should have been recognized and documented

5. Projects should be reviewed by senior management on a periodic basis and the views of project stakeholders should be sought regarding the project progress

6. Projects should submit regular progress reports, with some measure of their planned and actual performance on budget and timescale

7. The organization should recognize the projects they are undertaking and the reasons for them

If any of the above measures are not in place for all projects in the organization then steps should be taken to implement them before moving to level two.

Program Management Awareness

The program management awareness process area defines a common and agreed understanding within an organization about what program management involves. The organization does not have to carry out any programs, it should just understand what they are. This can be confirmed using the following steps:

1 Senior management understand the concept of program management as the coordination, direction and implementation of a collection of projects and activities that together achieve outcomes and realize benefits that are of strategic importance to the organization

2 Senior management recognize that major change can be complex and risky and that the breakdown of such initiatives into manageable chunks with review points for monitoring progress and assessing performance helps minimize risk

3 Senior management understand that programs can help the organization integrate and reconcile competing demands for resources and provide a focus for projects

4 Senior management are aware that programs should focus on outcomes rather than outputs and that program outcomes are perceived and described in terms of a vision for the program

5 Any programs that are run are reviewed by senior management on a periodic basis and the projects within a program are subject to regular review to confirm alignment with the program

If any of the above are lacking in the organization, they should be addressed before moving to level two.

Although there is an understanding of projects at this level, they are still run in isolation and there is only an awareness of programs. The next four topics step through the levels of maturity, listing the key process areas that need to be implemented.

Hot tip

Even if you are not intending to implement program management, senior management should be aware of the processes involved.

Level 2: Repeatable

For an organization to be rated at level 2, there are a further 11 key process areas that need to be implemented:

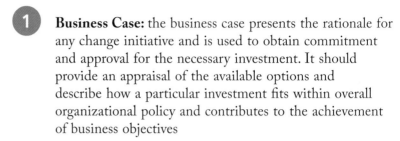

1 **Business Case:** the business case presents the rationale for any change initiative and is used to obtain commitment and approval for the necessary investment. It should provide an appraisal of the available options and describe how a particular investment fits within overall organizational policy and contributes to the achievement of business objectives

2 **Program Organization:** establishes the optimum organization for a program, defining the roles required, the responsibilities of each of these roles and the management structures and reporting arrangements needed to deliver the program's desired outcomes

Hot tip

Program organization (step 2) and program definition (step 3) can be skipped if you are not implementing program management.

3 **Program Definition:** sets out the specific needs for a program and its management. It involves the planning and design of all aspects of a program. It is a crucial process in that it provides the basis for deciding whether or not to proceed with a program

4 **Project Establishment:** defines the specific requirement for a project team and its management. It involves understanding the requirements in sufficient detail to profile the skills and competencies needed to perform the project activities. Profiles can then be used to identify individuals able to fulfil specific roles

5 **Project Planning, Monitoring and Control:** establishes how the project will be planned (work estimates developed to establish the resources required) and communicated to the project stakeholders. Monitoring and control provide visibility into project progress so that project or program management can take effective actions if the project's performance deviates from plan. It involves tracking and reviewing project accomplishments against estimates and plans, and revising plans based on actual accomplishments and results

6 **Stakeholder Management:** to understand stakeholders' interest in programs and projects and the impact a program or project will have on them. This then allows the implementation of a strategy to address their issues and needs

7 **Requirements Management:** establishes a common understanding between the program or project team and stakeholders concerning the business needs to be addressed by the program or project

8 **Risk Management:** to identify, analyze and avoid, minimize or control the adverse effects associated with risks that materialize. The risks may affect not only programs or projects but also the business generally and may need to be escalated to the appropriate business managers or stakeholders for action

9 **Configuration Management:** establishes and maintains the integrity of documentation and other deliverables, so the impact of any proposed changes can be assessed

10 **Program Planning and Control:** to combine various planning and monitoring activities within the approach documented in the program plan. Program planning is a continual activity throughout a program, focusing on the interdependencies between projects and dependencies on external factors

11 **Supplier Management:** to ensure they are selected and managed effectively. Management involves the establishment of mutual commitments, monitoring of both performance and results. Suppliers, partners and other parties may be selected based on strategic business alliances, as well as program and project considerations

Once these 11 areas (or eight if you are not implementing program management) have been implemented, the organization will have established repeatable P3M maturity.

Hot tip

Program planning and control (step 10) can also be skipped if you are not implementing program management.

Level 3: Defined

In order to be rated at level 3, there are a further 12 key process areas that an organization needs to implement:

1 **Benefits Management:** this involves the identification, planning, assignment of responsibility for the realization of and tracking the actual benefits of the business change as defined in the business case

2 **Transition Management:** to ensure the relevant business operations are prepared for the implementation of the project outputs. The transition plan sets out what needs to be done to ensure that the business environment is ready to exploit the new capability when it is delivered

3 **Information Management:** defines how the organization plans, collects, organizes, uses, controls, disseminates, archives and eventually disposes of all the information created during the project and program processes, to ensure that the potential value of information is identified and exploited

4 **Organizational Focus:** to establish responsibilities for program and project management activities so that they become standardized and fully integrated into the organization's business processes

5 **Process Definition:** to develop and maintain a set of program and project management processes that can be used by all programs and projects within the organization to improve project and program performance. This would include the definition of the organization's standard program and project management processes, frameworks, life cycle descriptions, templates and guidelines together with portfolio documentation libraries

6 **Training and Competency Development:** to develop the skills and knowledge of program and project managers, their teams and other personnel so they can perform their roles more effectively

7 **Integrated Management and Reporting:** the development of program and project plans that address the specific outcomes being sought by the business. Plans should be based on defined processes and describe how activities will be implemented, managed and reported on

8 **Life Cycle Control:** to ensure that the activities necessary to design, build and maintain the desired outputs are accomplished using the appropriate tools and methods, and that the process of transformation is conducted economically so that value can be demonstrated

9 **Inter-group Coordination:** establishing the means for teams to communicate and engage with other teams in order to satisfy the business and customer needs in an efficient and effective manner

10 **Quality Assurance:** to provide organizational assurance that programs and projects have suitable quality plans and measures in place to ensure that their deliverables meet explicit quality criteria. Quality assurance augments quality control in ensuring that quality is planned and built into programs and projects

11 **Centre of Excellence:** to establish a coordinating function providing strategic oversight, scrutiny and challenge across an organization's entire portfolio (this will become the portfolio office)

12 **Portfolio Establishment:** creation of the organization's portfolio of programs, projects and supporting processes to enable top management to make key decisions by building a single comprehensive picture of all the programs and projects in the portfolio

Once these 12 areas have been implemented the organization has established portfolio management maturity. Many organizations may choose to stop at this level but there is still a significant benefit in moving towards level four.

Hot tip

If not implementing portfolio management these last two steps can be skipped.

Level 4: Managed

In order to be rated at level four, there are a further four key process areas that an organization needs to implement:

1 **Management Metrics:** project and program management metrics need to be established in order to monitor the performance outcome from each process. To achieve this the organization will need to establish performance goals, collect process performance data from programs and projects and use this data to provide feedback on the likely outcome from the specified program and project approaches

2 **Quality Management:** to develop an understanding of the quality of program and project deliverables and the achievement of the organization's quality goals. To achieve this the organization will need to plan program and project quality assurance activities and define measurable goals for quality, then quantify and measure actual progress in achieving these goals

3 **Organizational Culture:** to recognize and address any barriers to successful change implementation in the organization. This requires identifying the current organizational culture and determine the climate required to improve the effectiveness of change initiatives. The organization will need to promote personnel development and organization flexibility in relation to the business environment, management control and governance

4 **Capacity Management:** to ensure that the organization has the necessary resources to meet the ongoing and future demands of the business in a cost effective manner. To achieve, this the organization will need to understand the business needs and the resource implications of the projects and programs needed to implement them

Once these four areas have been implemented, the organization will have established a good level of project, program and portfolio management maturity. But there is still a significant benefit in moving towards level five and continuous process improvement.

Beware

An organization's culture is what it does, not what it says it does!

Level 5: Optimizing

In order to be rated at level five, there are a final three key process areas that an organization needs to implement:

1 **Problem Management:** to identify potential problems in the program and project processes and to prevent them occurring. The underlying causes of program and project issues need to be identified and changes to the processes carried out to minimize the likelihood of future recurrence. To achieve this, the organization will need to plan proactive problem management activities, seek and identify common causes of program and project issues and problems and prioritize and systematically address all of them

2 **Technology Management:** to identify new technologies (techniques, tools and methods) and manage their implementation into the organization. To achieve this, the organization will need to evaluate new technologies in order to determine their potential effect on quality and productivity, plan the incorporation of any beneficial technology changes and ensure the release of these to the organization for embedding into standard program and project processes

3 **Continuous Process Improvement:** to continually improve the processes used in the organization with the intent of improving program and project quality, increasing productivity and decreasing life cycle times. To achieve this, the organization will need to plan continuous process improvement, ensure that participation in program and project process improvement initiatives is organization-wide and ensure that the organization's standard program and project processes are continuously improved

Once these three areas have been implemented the organization will have achieved optimizing level five and will continue to improve. Continuous process improvement is the key area and the one that defines an optimized organization. This will be next to impossible to achieve without some form of project, program and portfolio office to run and support the process improvement. This is covered in the next topic.

P3 Office

The establishment of a project, program and portfolio (P3) Office is key to the development of the organization's project, program and portfolio management maturity.

Once implemented, senior managers will have a high-level view of the portfolio, its progress, risks and benefits realization against investments. It will provide assistance in improving project, program and portfolio management through implementing best practice backed up with training and advice. The office will bring together in one place a set of principles, processes and techniques to facilitate effective project, program and portfolio management. It should, in short, become a centre of excellence.

Benefits

The main benefit to the organization will be in the bottom line as with a project, program and portfolio management office in place:

- The right programs and projects will be selected on the basis of strategic alignment and benefits delivery

- Prioritization will result in the optimum number of programs and projects being initiated to meet strategic goals, within the available capacity of the organization

- Programs and projects will be carried out in the right way, with every success or failure visible so that problems can be escalated to the right level and judgments made

- Senior management will be assisted with decision making on strategic alignment, prioritization, risk and optimization of resources to successfully deliver their business objectives

- Knowledge management will ensure improving estimating, planning and implementation with fewer mistakes

- The office will add value by providing expert challenge, decision support and improved understanding of organizational investment

- A strategic approach to risk will be understood, leading to appropriate levels of risk taking

- Program management standards will be tailored to organizational needs, leading to appropriate application of best practice and greater program control

- Business cases will be independently validated for achievability and the organization's capability to deliver them

- Roles and responsibilities within the program and project teams will be well defined, understood and communicated, with the added value of the office acknowledged

- The culture will become outcome and benefits focused, ensuring that projects deliver outputs that will enable benefits to be achieved

- There will be a better overview of progress and delivery against plan with strong financial controls

- There will be assurance and review of project delivery and compliance with project management standards

- The organization will be able to balance change initiatives with business as usual

Implementing P3 Office

The steps required to implement project, program and portfolio offices are covered at the end of the three preceding chapters. Implementing a project, program and portfolio (P3) office is best carried out in the following sequence:

1 Set up a project office using the steps listed on page 35 and ensure that all projects comply with the standard processes and methods

2 Once the project office is functioning successfully, add the program office functions to it (or set up a separate program office) using the steps listed on page 57 and ensure all programs are compliant

3 Once the program office is functioning successfully, add the portfolio office functions (or set up a separate portfolio office) using the steps listed on page 75

Implementing the P3 office in this structured way will ensure its success as each level builds on an established foundation provided by the previous step. You will also be developing a pool of people who understand the processes involved.

Hot tip

If you are not intending to implement program management then step 2 can be skipped.

Summary

- Any organization carrying out project, program or portfolio management should aspire to reach at least level three (defined) in terms of the related maturity, by implementing the supporting processes

- The benefit is that mature organizations typically have a lower cost of managing projects (almost half the cost) and much lower project failure rate

- OPM3 and P3M3 are two methodologies that can be used to develop project, program and portfolio maturity but they are not essential to the process

- The first step is to rate your organization's level of project management maturity and if it is at level three or below draw up a plan to improve it to level four (managed)

- Level one (initial) of the combined project, program and portfolio management maturity model assumes two key process areas are in place: project definition and program management awareness

- Level two (repeatable) adds 11 further key process areas including: the business case, program organization, program definition, project establishment, stakeholder management, requirements management and risk management

- Level three (defined) adds a further 12 process areas including: benefits management, transition management, training and competency development, life cycle control and portfolio establishment

- Level four (managed) adds: management metrics, quality management, organizational culture and capacity management

- Level five (optimizing) adds: problem management, technology management and continuous process improvement (this last area being key to optimizing)

- Establishing a project, program and portfolio office (P3 Office) is best carried out in three steps: establishing a project office, adding the program office functions to it and then adding the portfolio office functions. This will ensure that each step is built on a firm foundation

6 Implementing Program Management

This chapter explains how to go about implementing program management in an organization and the key processes that need to be in place to support it.

Introduction

Program management can be implemented with or without the implementation of portfolio management (and vice-versa). The only impact on program management is to whom the program board report. If portfolio management is in place, then it is to the portfolio manager, if not it is to the group within the business that have sponsored the program.

Precursors

Program management is increasingly being recognized as a key tool in enabling organizations to deliver their strategy and manage the change process required. However, the successful implementation of program management in an organization does require having a number of key factors and processes in place:

1. **Organizational Maturity:** in order to implement program management, there must be at least a basic level of organizational project management maturity in place (organizational maturity was covered in Chapter 5 and there is a summary of the process in on page 100)

2. **Program Office:** as with organizational maturity, there is a basic requirement for a program office to support program management. It is unlikely to exist if no programs have been carried out in the organization. However, there should, at the very least, be a project office established and the program office can be developed from this group

3. **Governance:** program governance is always most effective when aligned with existing corporate governance, and while this may take a little longer, it will repay the effort required to achieve it

4. **Program Organization:** the management structure, reporting and responsibilities should be defined in order to expedite the start up of programs

5. **Organizational Vision:** the vision statement is a key document in ensuring programs are aligned to the strategy of the organization. It should set out the desired future state of the organization

6 **Stakeholder Engagement:** is crucial to program management and the organization should have a documented policy on this topic

7 **Benefits Management:** is another key element of program management and, again, the organization needs to have a clear definition and understanding of benefits management and realization

8 **Planning and Control:** processes, again, need to be clearly defined and robust, as they are key to the success of any change program

9 **Business Case:** a clearly defined standard for setting out the business case for any change program or project should exist together with the processes required to support it

10 **Risk and Issue Management:** processes must be defined for the identification, management and mitigation of risks and issues

11 **Quality Management:** again the organizational standards for quality management and assurance need to be documented

These factors and processes are described, with guidelines on their implementation, in the remainder of this chapter. Once they have been defined and implemented, the organization will be ready for the implementation of program management.

Implementing Program Management
To be truly effective, program management needs to be embedded in the organization. This means it must be a part of the overall management structure of the organization and must reflect a consistent approach to culture, roles and processes. The whole process of implementing program management is likely to be a significant organizational change, which itself may require a change project (or program) to implement it.

Organizational Maturity

As we saw in the previous chapter, there are five levels of the combined project, program and portfolio management maturity model that an organization passes through as it seeks to achieve and then improve on its best practices. It addresses the maturity of an organization in its ability to manage projects, programs and portfolios from a process perspective. The following table provides a questionnaire to identify the current level of project and program management maturity:

Maturity	Project Management	Program Management
Level 1: Initial	Does the organization recognize projects and run them differently from its ongoing business?	Does the organization recognize programs and run them differently from projects?
Level 2: Repeatable	Does the organization ensure each project is run with its own processes and procedures to a minimum specified standard?	Does the organization ensure each program is run with its own processes and procedures to a minimum specified standard?
Level 3: Defined	Does the organization have its own centrally controlled project processes and can individual projects flex within these processes to suit the project?	Does the organization have its own centrally controlled program processes and can individual programs flex within these processes to suit the program?
Level 4: Managed	Does the organization obtain and retain specific measures of its project management performance and run a quality management organization to better predict future performance?	Does the organization obtain and retain specific measures of its program management performance and run a quality management organization to better predict future program outcomes?
Level 5: Optimizing	Does the organization run continuous process improvement, with proactive problem and technology management for projects in order to improve its ability to predict performance over time and optimize processes?	Does the organization run continuous process improvement, with proactive problem and technology management for programs in order to improve its ability to predict performance over time and optimize processes?

To begin implementing program management effectively, an organization should be at least at level three for project management and level one for program management.

Project Management Improvement

In terms of project management maturity, unless the organization is already at level 4 (managed) or 5 (optimizing), an action plan needs to be developed to improve the project management maturity. It is only feasible and realistic to aim for improving by one level at a time. Follow that improvement by a review and then plan for the next level of improvement.

Details of the recommended project management improvement process are set out on page 85.

Program Management Improvement

In order to implement program management successfully, an action plan needs to be created to develop and improve the organization's program management maturity. The following steps are recommended for this:

1 Level 1 (initial) requires just two factors to be in place: a clear understanding of what a project is and an awareness of what a program is and how it differs from a project (see pages 86 to 87)

2 To move to level 2 (repeatable) requires the identification and documentation of program management processes and standards (see pages 88 to 89)

3 Moving to level 3 (defined) requires an established program office supported by several more documented key processes (see pages 90 to 91)

4 Moving on to level 4 (managed) and level 5 (optimizing) should by this stage be driven by the program office itself

Adopting and developing program management maturity will take time. The organization will want to plan how it evolves and should set itself improvement targets to the next level, with regular progress and process reviews.

Program Office

Typically, an organization moving into program management will add the program office functions to an already functioning project office, creating a combined program and project office. Program and project offices have a variety of important roles, but this does not necessarily mean that they must be located in the same physical area. Program and project offices can be combined or separate, they may be in the same or different locations, there may be multiple project offices or they could even be virtual and provided by individuals in different locations.

The following diagram illustrates the position of the program office within the program management structure (titles may vary from organization to organization):

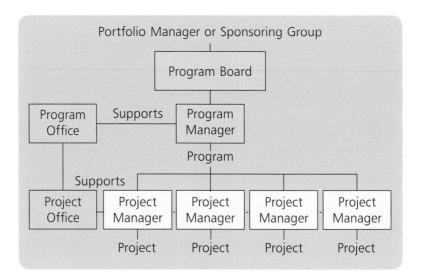

A successfully implemented program office can act as the conscience and support body for the program board. It can also provide advice and challenge on what decisions the program board need to take.

It can provide administration, technical expertise (such as planning or risk management), specialist activities such as the use of program and project management tools and training to the program team.

Guidelines for the implementation of a program office were covered, step-by-step (on page 57).

Governance

Governance refers to the control framework through which programs deliver their change objectives and remain within corporate visibility and control. A program needs clear and open governance if it is to be successful.

Integrating Governance

The governance mechanisms in a program are most effective when integrated with the corporate governance already used in an organization. This will enable programs to be aligned with the business culture. Integrated governance can be achieved using the following steps:

1 Stakeholder engagement strategy and methods should be developed and integrated with the organization's corporate communications functions

2 Program risk management strategy should be derived from and directly reference the corporate risk approach (risk management policy, process guidance and strategy)

3 Quality strategy should support and enhance the corporate quality management standards and processes (e.g. if the organization is compliant with an ISO standard, then program quality should incorporate that)

4 Information management strategy should reflect and integrate with corporate information policies, templates and storage systems rather than develop its own; it should also fit with any appropriate reporting cycles

5 Resource management plans should utilize procurement frameworks and supplier relationships wherever possible and take advantage of the negotiating power of the organization with suppliers

This approach may take a little longer to establish due to the broader stakeholder engagement and flexibility required but, by drawing on this internal expertise and established standards, the program will be better established and reduce the likelihood of conflict within the organization.

Program Organization

The following diagram illustrates the program management organization. The program board reports to the sponsoring group (or portfolio manager if portfolio management is implemented). Portfolio management is covered in later chapters so for the purpose of this chapter we will assume that the program board reports into a sponsoring group.

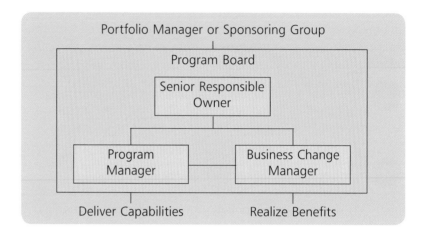

Program Board

The program board is responsible for driving the program in order to deliver the required capability and realize the benefits. It consists of the senior responsible owner (SRO) who also chairs the board, the program manager and the business change manager. In addition, it may also include relevant representatives of project boards, the project office, corporate functions and suppliers.

Senior Responsible Owner

The SRO will be a member of and is appointed by the sponsoring group. They will be accountable to the sponsoring group for the program, ensuring it meets its objectives and realizes the expected benefits. They must have enough seniority to provide leadership to the program team and take on accountability for delivery.

Program Manager

The program manager is responsible for leading and managing the program from its initial set up, through the delivery of new capabilities and realization of benefits to program closure. The program manager has primary responsibility for successful delivery of the new capabilities and establishing program governance.

Business Change Manager

While the program manager has prime responsibility for delivery of new capabilities, the business change manager (BCM) has prime responsibility for realizing the resultant benefits. They are responsible for embedding the new capabilities into the business operations and facilitating business changes to exploit those new capabilities.

The individuals appointed to these two roles must be able to work in close partnership to ensure that the right capabilities are delivered and put to best use in the business.

If a program is implementing change across different parts of the organization, each should nominate a BCM. They may all be members of the program board or they may have one representative on the board. Each BCM may also be supported by a business change team.

Sponsoring Group

The sponsoring group (which could be an existing executive group) consists of senior managers with responsibility for the strategic direction of the organization, the business investment decision and ensuring the program stays aligned with that strategic direction. They have overall authority over the program but will delegate a significant portion of this (with any limits) to the SRO. They will, however, still be formally involved with:

1 Authorizing the organization's strategic direction against which the program is to deliver

2 Appointing, advising and supporting the SRO

3 Authorizing the program mandate, definition and vision statement

4 Authorizing funding for the program

5 Providing commitment and endorsement to the program

6 Authorizing delivery and sign-off at the closure of the program

Hot tip

In a smaller organization some of these roles may be combined but the board should always be at least two people for good governance.

Key Processes

In addition to the key factors and processes listed as precursors at the start of this chapter, there are a further seven key processes that need to be developed for effective program management:

1 **Organizational Vision:** the program vision statement describes the innovations and improvements the program will deliver in line with the organizational vision; therefore, there must be an organizational vision statement, which describes the desired future state of the organization and a process which supports its use

2 **Stakeholder Engagement:** stakeholders are the individuals or groups who will be impacted by or can have an impact on the program and who may support or oppose the change. In either event they need to be involved as they are likely to become helpful or unhelpful, depending on how they themselves are influenced; therefore, there needs to be an established process for stakeholder engagement

3 **Benefits Management:** this is at the very heart of program management as programs are driven by the need to deliver benefits and this is achieved through the constituent projects delivering outcomes that realize benefits for the organization. But realization of benefits actually takes place in the operational area of the business after the program has delivered new capabilities to the business operations, and may not happen until long after the program has been completed. Therefore, there needs to be an established process for benefits management

4 **Planning and Control:** are both key to the success of any change program and they are complementary activities. Development of the program plan involves processing large amounts of information and extensive consultation; program control provides supporting activities and processes that run throughout the life cycle of the program to refine and improve delivery and justify the continuance of the program. There should be established processes, based on and updated as a result of experience from earlier program phases

Hot tip

The program vision document is a key document for obtaining stakeholder buy in.

5   **Business Case:** the program board and sponsoring group must have confidence that the program is still viable, desirable and achievable as it progresses. The business case provides the benchmark that is used to test the viability of the program. It has to be maintained throughout the program and continually updated with new information on benefits, costs, risks and the timescale for achievement. There must be an established process in place to support the development and updating of the business case

6   **Risk and Issue Management:** risks and issues can occur at any time during a program and must be managed. Risk management is the process of identifying and then mitigating risks that could impact the program's achievement of outcomes or realization of expected benefits. Issue management is the process used for dealing with events that have happened, were not planned and require management actions. There needs to be an established process in place to ensure the adequate management of program risks and issues

7   **Quality Management:** sometimes regarded as the poor relation of program management, quality management is necessary to ensure that all management aspects of the program are working appropriately and that it stays on target to achieve its objectives. Quality management at the program level is different from quality management at the project level; as in a program the focus is on management processes, alignment with corporate strategy and the environment within which it exists. Again, there needs to be an established program quality management process in place to ensure this happens

Some or all of these processes may already be established in the organization, but they will not necessarily be defined to cover program management. The most straightforward way of developing them is to task the program office (once it has been set up) with developing suitable processes from new (or from existing corporate or project processes) to cover these key process areas.

An organization's culture is what it does, not what it says it does!

Beware

These specialists need to be handled with care or they may become negative stakeholders!

Implementation

The introduction and implementation of program management in an organization is a significant change in itself and should be treated as a project (or possibly even a program) in its own right. There are a number of topics that will need to be addressed, starting with the culture of the organization.

Top Management

Effective implementation of program management will require the backing and commitment of the senior management of the organization. This will require top executive or board-level sponsorship with full visibility and engagement with sponsoring groups, program boards and any other involved parties.

Organizational Competence

Knowledge and awareness of program management is required across the entire organization, not just in the project management community. All disciplines and functions should be engaged and committed. Operations managers need to be fully aware of program and project management procedures and terminology to enable them to contribute effectively to the outcomes of change projects as they are implemented.

Specialist Roles

In addition to top management's role, there are a number of specialist roles that can prove valuable in supporting the adoption of program management:

- Appoint program management 'champions' in each of the business areas that will be impacted by programs, who will promote program management awareness

- Inclusion of change delivery objectives for key operational line management staff in areas that will be impacted by programs, with links to the realization of benefits

- In addition to the standard roles within a program structure, there may also be benefit in defining roles for nominated individuals to cover areas such as:

  - Risk and issue management

  - Benefits management

  - Planning

- Communications

- Quality management

- Change and configuration control

Implementation Process

A key part of the implementation process is the staff training, education and awareness. This needs to be supported by documented processes, procedures, standards and guidelines. The following should form the outline for an implementation plan:

1 Ensure that the organization has sufficient process maturity and a program office is established (covered on pages 54 to 57)

2 Document a standard program life cycle, supported by standard processes (which cover the key process areas), methods and guidelines for running programs (see pages 50 to 51)

3 Obtain top management commitment and support for the use of these processes and methods

4 Develop suitable tools and templates, which will enable consistency and will drive best practice throughout the business

5 Produce a training program to ensure all relevant staff are familiar with the life cycle, approach, processes, methods, tools and templates

6 Ensure that quality assurance activities are built into the program office to maintain a focus on process efficiency and continuous process improvement

7 Select a pilot program (if one has not already self-selected or triggered the implementation of program management) and the organization will be ready to start up and run a program (which is covered in the next chapter)

Summary

- Program management can be implemented with or without portfolio management, the only impact is whether the program board report to the portfolio manager or business sponsoring group

- The successful implementation of program management in an organization requires a basic level of organizational maturity and a program or project office

- To be truly effective, program management needs to be embedded in the organization; this requires a consistent approach to culture, roles and processes

- To begin implementing program management effectively an organization should be at least at level three for project management and level one for program management maturity

- A program office can act as the conscience and support body for the program board and provide administration, technical expertise and training to the program team

- Program governance is most effective when integrated with the corporate governance already used in the organization, to enable programs to be aligned with the business culture

- The program board is responsible for driving the program to deliver the capability and realize the benefits. The core members are: the senior responsible owner, the program manager and the business change manager

- There are seven key processes that need to be in place to support program management: organizational vision, stakeholder engagement, benefits management, planning and control, business case, risk and issue management and quality management

- The implementation of program management in an organization is a significant change and should be treated as a project (or possibly even a program) in its own right

- Successful implementation of program management is dependant on top management support, creation of standards, processes, methods, documentation and tools, supported by a program of awareness and training

7 Managing a Program

This chapter examines what is involved in managing a program through the phases and stages from start up to close out.

Introduction

We looked at the program life cycle in Chapter 3 and defined three phases and seven stages as illustrated below:

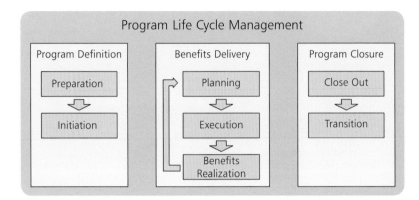

In this chapter we will be looking at what is involved in managing the three phases and their constituent stages.

1 **Program Definition** involves understanding the strategic value of the program, defining the program objectives, identifying the key stakeholders and decision makers, developing a high level business case for the program, obtaining approval for the program and appointing the program manager

2 **Benefits Delivery** represents the main ongoing program management activity and for each of the constituent projects this will entail planning, execution and benefits realization. For the program as a whole it also involves managing the inter-project dependencies, risks and issues

3 **Program Closure** performs a controlled close down of the program, together with the shutdown of the program infrastructure and transition of benefits monitoring to an operational group

These three phases and the constituent stages are covered in the remainder of this chapter. There are a number of key terms that feature in this chapter and in several other parts of the book that it will be helpful to define:

Program

A program is a temporary organizational structure, created in order to direct, coordinate and oversee the implementation of a set of related projects and other activities, in order to deliver benefits in line with the organization's strategic objectives.

A program will usually have a life span of several years while a project will typically have a life span of a year or less.

Benefits

Benefits are measurable improvements to the business achieved by the outcomes of the projects in the program. They are achieved by the operational groups responsible for managing the changed operational procedures introduced by the program.

Program Vision

The program vision is a crucial statement that must be relevant to and aligned with corporate objectives, mission statements, strategies, policies and any other relevant documents.

Program Governance

Program governance refers to the mechanisms and processes implemented to monitor and control the program. Again, these mechanisms and processes must be aligned to and integrated with corporate governance already used within the organization.

Stakeholder Engagement

Active engagement with all program stakeholders is critical to the success of program management. This is not just a matter of sending them emails or reports, it must involve creating a proper relationship with face-to-face communication if possible.

Risk and Issue Management

Risks represent unplanned events that could have a detrimental impact on the program. Issues are risks (identified or not) that have happened and had an impact on the program. Both need to be managed following organizational standards.

Resource Management

One of the drivers for program management is the effective use of resources between the constituent projects. But moving people about can have a negative impact on the projects affected so this needs careful management.

Preparation

Preparation is the first stage of the program definition phase. Before a program can be started formally, it has to go through a series of pre-program processes and activities:

Selection

First, a program has to be identified by someone or some body within the organization. This should be as a result of some business need, either to address a change initiative that would be too large for a single project, or as a result of identifying several proposed or active projects that have sufficient dependencies to justify grouping them into a program. The result of this should be some sort of program proposal that will go to the appropriate authority for approval. The steps in this process are:

1 Define the strategic objectives that the program is designed to address, the objectives of the program and how it is aligned with the strategic objectives

2 Identify the key decision makers and stakeholders who should be involved in the approval process, with their expectations and interests

3 Develop a high level business case for the program that addresses the need, cost/benefit justification, feasibility of the program and why a program is needed as opposed to a single project or several separate projects

Why a Program?

The business case will need to justify the additional costs and overheads of the program, this may include:

- The program is too large to be treated as a project and the component projects are too interdependent to be treated as separate unrelated projects

- Optimizing the use of scarce resources by sharing them across several related projects in the program

- Keeping the projects aligned with strategic goals and benefits

- Dealing with inter-project dependencies and coordinating involvement with different parts of the organization

…cont'd

There are several more steps that need to be carried out:

4   Select an appropriate program manager

5   Develop a high level business plan for the program and a more detailed plan for the initiation of the program

6   Obtain the support of the key stakeholders to the proposal and plan by getting their sign off to the strategic objectives and business case

7   Submit the proposal to the appropriate authority for approval

Selection Criteria

Due to the strategic nature and size of programs, they will normally need to be authorized at a high level in an organization. This may be an executive board, portfolio manager, program board, or some other senior body. Whatever the selection process, the criteria are likely to be similar:

● **Strategic fit:** how well the program fits with the business strategy of the organization

● **Benefits analysis:** what the benefits to the business are and how they will be achieved

● **Budget:** the preliminary budget estimate for the program

● **Resources:** the human and other resources required for the program and their availability

● **Risks:** an analysis of the potential risks to the program

Program Approval

If the program is approved, it moves on to the initiation stage with the appointment of the program manager, issuing of the program charter (program vision, key objectives, expected benefits, assumptions and constraints) and the approved plan (including key resources needed and committed) for the initiation stage.

If the program is not approved, it goes back to the drawing board to be revised or is put on hold.

RAID is a useful acronym in the evaluation process, it stands for Risks, Assumptions, Issues and Dependencies.

Initiation

Initiation is the second part of the program definition phase and follows the successful approval of the proposed program. The two key activities in this phase are:

- Identifying the key deliverables from the program

- Developing a detailed plan (road map) for the program, giving the direction of the program, how it will be managed and how the key deliverables will be produced

Key Deliverables

The key deliverables are the results produced by the program that will bring about the expected benefits. The key deliverables must be identified so that they can be mapped onto the individual projects (including any intermediate enabling projects) which will deliver them.

Detailed Plan

The detailed program management plan will need to set out the road map for how the benefits of the program will be delivered:

1 Ensure the program's mission, values and vision are aligned with the organization's strategic objectives as defined in the business case

2 Develop a program architecture that shows how the individual components (projects) in the program will develop the capabilities that result in expected benefits set out in the business case

3 For each project in the program, develop a business case, the feasibility of the project, detailed costs, project plan and any constraints and assumptions

4 Assemble the overall program scope, plan and schedule from the individual component projects and any other supporting activities

5 Develop the cost estimates, budget, resource requirements, staff allocation, external resources and risk analysis for the program and identify the preliminary program team

6 Communicate with all program stakeholders to gain their support and approval for the detailed plan

7 Obtain approval for the plan

The detailed program management plan, as submitted for approval, should address the following:

- What the key deliverables from the program are and when they will be delivered

- What the overall cost of the program will be

- What risks there are to the program and any planned mitigation

- Any constraints, dependencies and assumptions

- How the program will be managed and run

Program Approval

The approval of the program proposal (as covered at the end of the previous topic) authorized this initiation stage. Now at the end of the initiation stage this second request is for approval to proceed to the main phase of the program: benefits delivery (the planning and execution of the program and benefits realization).

This approval will be based on the program management plan and the revised business case (updated following the development of the program management plan). These two key documents are complimentary in that:

- The business case sets out what the program is going to do, why it is doing it, the costs and the benefits

- The program management plan sets out how and when the program is going to deliver the benefits and how the program will be managed

This represents the final step in business approval for the program. After approval, the program proceeds to the benefits delivery phase, which is likely to span several years. Larger programs may be split up into several tranches (sub-phases) so that progress can be reviewed formally from time-to-time.

Program Infrastructure

The benefits delivery phase controls the planning, execution and benefits realization of each project in the program. It is a cyclical process that continues until the last project in the program has been completed.

Once the program definition phase has been completed and the program has been authorized; program planning, execution and benefits realization can, in theory, begin. However, there are four key things that need to be in place first:

1 **Program Governance:** to ensure the program meets the objectives and delivers the benefits

2 **Program Office:** to define the organizational program standards and support the program team

3 **Program Team:** to carry out the work of the program

4 **Program Facilities:** to provide the environment and tools to enable the program team to operate

Program Governance

In program governance (Chapter 3) and program organization (Chapter 6) we looked at the program management infrastructure, as illustrated below:

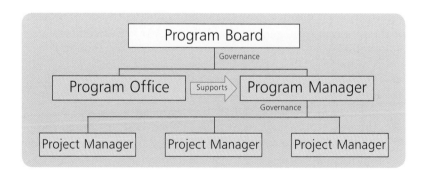

The program board is empowered by the organization to have governance over and make management decisions regarding the program. The program manager reports into the program board and clearly this needs to be set up if it is not already in place.

Appointments need to be made to the following roles:

- **Senior Responsible Owner:** (executive sponsor) has the primary responsibility for the delivery of the program benefits

- **Program Manager:** has day-to-day responsibility for the program

- **Business Change Manager:** responsible for embedding the new capabilities into the business as they are delivered

These roles were covered in more detail on pages 104 and 105. Once formed, the program board may then choose to co-opt other members as appropriate.

Program Office
The program office not only provides part of the governance of the program but it also supports the program manager and program board. Clearly this also needs to be set up (as covered on page 57) if it is not already in place.

Program Team
The program team consists of the program manager and any other required supporting team members together with the project managers of any active projects in the program.

Program Facilities
In addition to the management infrastructure there are a number of facilities, procedures and tools that will be required to support the program:

- **Facilities**: office space, equipment, storage and computer facilities

- **Procedures:** program specific standards, guidelines, processes and documentation standards and templates

- **Tools:** for resource management, planning, progress tracking, performance measurement and benefits tracking

- Together with any other technical material needed to support the program

Once these program facilities are in place the program is ready to begin planning, execution and benefits realization.

Benefits Delivery

The benefits delivery phase controls the planning, execution and benefits realization of each project in the program. It is a cyclical process (as illustrated below right) that continues until the last project in the program has been completed.

Project Governance

The first thing the program must do is establish project governance by planning how it will monitor and control the constituent projects. This will involve the following steps:

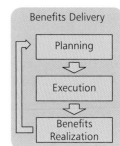

1 Initiation of the constituent projects

2 Ensure the project managers adhere to the organization's project management standards and methodology

3 Ensure the project deliverables meet the business and technical requirements

4 Track that project costs are within budget

5 Manage the communication, coordination and dependencies between projects and any other programs

6 Identify any changes that might impact the program plan or projected benefits

7 Review change requests and authorize any additional work required to implement them

8 Identify risks to the program, monitor them and plan any necessary responses

9 Identify program issues and ensure any necessary corrective actions are taken

10 Optimize the use of resources over the program and its constituent projects

11 Communicate with the program board and other stakeholders

Benefits Realization

The prime measure of program performance is in the benefits achieved against plan. Benefits realization is an ongoing, incremental process through the life of the program and beyond. Performance is measured through the following steps:

1 Review the efforts and performance of the constituent project teams against their project plans

2 Analyze the overall program performance against the program plan

3 Monitor the actual delivery of benefits against the program plan and if necessary take remedial action if the variance exceeds the agreed level of tolerance

Transition Management

Another ongoing task is the management of the transition of the business from the previous state to the planned future state. That is, from the actual performance to the expected performance.

Most of the steps listed on these two pages are repeated as often as is necessary to stay in control of the program. Many of these steps may be carried out by or with assistance from the program office. They continue until such time as the last constituent project of the program has been completed or the program is closed for some other reason.

Once this state has been reached, the program can move onto the final phase of program closure.

Program Closure

Permission to move onto program closure should be sought from and given by the program board. This should be a formal process to review the performance of the program against plan and the achievement of benefits to date against the business case. Normally, the benefits will not have been realized completely from the last few projects and this is dealt with in program closure.

Hot tip

Tolerance is a term used to define the agreed acceptable level of variation from budget on costs, benefits and time.

121

Program Closure

The program closure phase consists of two stages: program close out and transition. They will typically tend to overlap.

Close Out

The close out stage is concerned with shutting down the program infrastructure. It will typically involve the following steps:

1 Document the current status of the program and benefits delivery and review them with the program board, sponsoring group and all other key stakeholders

2 Check all contractual obligations have been met by suppliers, all bills paid and close all nominal accounts

3 Capture and document the lessons learned (both good and bad) during the program and store them in the program office database for the benefit of future programs

4 Review all changes made during the program and document their impact on the results of the program

5 Develop recommendations based on experience for the results of the program and the processes used

6 Index and archive all the relevant documents created during the program, so that they are available for future programs to use

7 Ensure that the redeployment of human resources has been arranged and disband the program team

8 Ensure that arrangements have been made for the redeployment of physical resources and dismantle the program infrastructure

The guiding principle for close out is that future programs run by the organization will be able to benefit from everything learnt on this program. The lessons learned will allow the organization to benefit from best practices and improve on problem areas.

Transition

Each individual project within the program will have transferred the project's artefacts to the appropriate operations group, this stage of program closure deals with the transfer of program artifacts and benefits monitoring to the appropriate ongoing operations groups. This will typically involve the following steps:

1 Program artefacts (physical objects produced by the program) should be transferred to the appropriate operations or support group

2 Transfer operational responsibility for any ongoing program operations to the appropriate operations or support group

3 Transfer benefits monitoring responsibility to the appropriate operations group for ongoing benefits realization and reporting

4 Capture and document any further lessons learned from these steps and deal with these as part of close out

5 Formally close the program

Benefits Realization

Although some benefits will have been realized during the program, there is usually a significant lag between implementing a project and the full realization of the benefits delivered.

As part of the transfer of benefits responsibility to an operational group, the details for future assessment of benefits realization will need to be spelled out clearly. Normally, the responsibility for benefits realization will be transferred to the operational group responsible for the new business operations. However, it may be that this realization activity will be managed as a separate piece of work, possibly even as a project.

Whoever is taking over responsibility, the transition process will need to be accompanied by documentation and support to allow the receiving group to take over the relevant responsibilities in an effective manner.

Summary

Program Definition
The first phase of a program consists of:

- **Preparation:** which covers selection of the program, selection of a program manager, development of a high level business plan, obtaining stakeholder support and authorization

- **Initiation:** deals with identification of the key deliverables and development of the detailed program plan, again followed by obtaining stakeholder support and authorization

- Once the program has been authorized the program infrastructure can be put in place, including program governance, program office, setting up the program team and any supporting facilities required

Benefits Delivery
The benefits delivery phase takes place through the execution of the constituent projects in the program and consists of:

- **Planning:** initiating and defining how each project will be monitored and controlled

- **Execution:** overseeing the successful execution of the constituent projects and the business transition to the new ongoing operations

- **Benefits Realization:** measurement of the benefits achieved by the business organization through the new operations

Program Closure
Once all the projects in the program have been completed the program can be closed down:

- **Close Out:** review the program, capture the lessons learned and arrange the redeployment of the human and physical resources used on the program

- **Transition:** transfer the program artefacts and responsibility for ongoing benefits realization

- **Benefits Realization:** will continue for some time after the end of the program and this needs to be managed until all of the benefits from the program can be confirmed and compared to the expected benefits

8 Implementing Portfolio Management

This chapter explains how to go about implementing portfolio management in an organization and the key processes that need to be in place to support it.

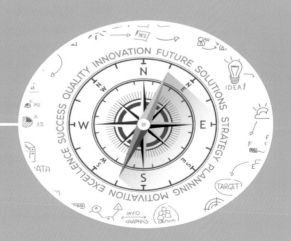

Introduction

Portfolio management can be implemented with or without the implementation of program management. This choice will largely depend on the size of the organization and the size of the projects it carries out. However, with or without program management, portfolio management can bring significant benefits.

Precursors

Put at its simplest, portfolio management is about making the best decisions about which projects to carry out with the human and financial resources available in the organization and tracking the return on investment of those projects. However, to implement it successfully in an organization, there are a number of factors that need to be in place:

1. **Organizational Maturity:** in order to implement portfolio management, there must be at least a basic level of organizational project management maturity in place (organizational maturity was covered in Chapter 5 and there is a summary of the process on page 128)

2. **Portfolio Office:** unless it is a small organization, there will probably be a requirement for a portfolio office to support the portfolio manager. This will not exist prior to implementing portfolio management. However, there should at the very least be a project office established and the portfolio office can be developed from this group

3. **Governance:** project and portfolio governance are always most effective when aligned with existing corporate governance and while this may take a little longer, it will repay the effort required to achieve it

4. **Organizational Vision:** the vision statement is a key document in ensuring the portfolio is aligned to the strategy of the organization. It should set out the desired future state of the organization

5. **Stakeholder Engagement:** is crucial to portfolio management and the organization should have a stakeholder management approach that encourages it

6   **Benefits Management:** is another key element of portfolio management and, again, the organization needs to have a clear definition of benefits management and realization

7   **Planning and Control:** processes need, again, to be clearly defined as they are key to the success of portfolio management

8   **Business Case:** a clearly defined standard for setting out the business case for any project or program should exist, together with the processes required to support it

9   **Risk and Issue Management:** processes must be defined for the identification, management and mitigation of risks and issues for projects, programs and the portfolio

10   **Senior Management Commitment:** portfolio management involves the active participation and support of the organization's top management; they, therefore, need a good understanding of project management and feedback on current and historical project performance

At the portfolio level, risks can be thought of as chances that can have good or bad outcomes.

These factors and processes are described, with guidelines on their implementation, in the remainder of this chapter. Once they have been defined and implemented (or are ready for implementation), the organization will be ready to move ahead with the implementation of portfolio management.

Senior Management

Without a doubt the most critical of the factors listed above is the final one, senior management commitment. Ideally they should already be aware of the return on investment achieved by projects in the past and understand the potential benefits of introducing portfolio management.

To be truly effective, portfolio management needs to be embedded in the organization. This will require a consistent approach to culture, roles and processes, which itself may require a change project or program to implement it.

Organizational Maturity

As we saw in Chapter 5, there are five levels to the combined project, program and portfolio management maturity model that an organization passes through as it seeks to achieve and then improve on its best practices. It addresses the maturity of an organization in its ability to manage projects, programs and portfolios from a process perspective. The following table provides a questionnaire to identify the current level of project and portfolio management maturity:

Maturity	Project Management	Portfolio Management
Level 1: Initial	Does the organization recognize projects and run them differently from its ongoing business?	Does the organization recognize projects and have an informal list of its investments in projects?
Level 2: Repeatable	Does the organization ensure each project is run with its own processes and procedures to a minimum specified standard?	Does the organization ensure each project is run with its own processes and procedures to a minimum specified standard?
Level 3: Defined	Does the organization have its own centrally controlled project processes and can individual projects flex within these processes to suit the project?	Does the organization have its own centrally controlled portfolio management processes?
Level 4: Managed	Does the organization obtain and retain specific measures of its project management performance and run a quality management organization to better predict future performance?	Does the organization assess its capacity to manage programs and projects and prioritize them accordingly?
Level 5: Optimizing	Does the organization run continuous process improvement, with proactive problem and technology management for projects in order to improve its ability to predict performance over time and optimize processes?	Does the organization run continuous process improvement, with proactive problem and technology management for the portfolio, in order to improve its ability to predict performance over time and optimize processes?

To begin implementing portfolio management effectively an organization should be at least at level three for project management and level one for portfolio management.

Project Management Improvement

In terms of project management maturity, unless the organization is already at level 4 (managed) or 5 (optimized), an action plan needs to be developed to improve the project management maturity. It is only feasible and realistic to aim for improving by one level at a time. Follow that improvement by a review and then plan for the next level of improvement.

Details of the recommended project management improvement process is set out on page 85.

Portfolio Management Improvement

In order to implement portfolio management successfully, an action plan needs to be developed to develop and then improve the organization's portfolio management maturity. The following steps are recommended for this:

1. Level 1 (initial) requires just two factors to be in place: a sound understanding of what a project is and an awareness of what a program and a portfolio are and how they differ from a project (see page 86)

2. To move to level 2 (repeatable) requires the identification and documentation of several project and program management processes and standards (see page 88)

3. Moving to level 3 (defined) requires the establishment of a portfolio office supported by several more documented key processes (see page 90)

4. Moving on to level 4 (managed) and level 5 (optimizing) should by this stage be driven by the portfolio office

Adopting and developing project and portfolio management maturity will take time. The organization will want to plan how it evolves and should set itself improvement targets to the next level, with regular reviews.

Hot tip

If the organization is not implementing program management, the relevant processes can be skipped.

Portfolio Office

There are basically two choices for creating a portfolio office: start from scratch or add the portfolio office functions to an already functioning project or program office. Project, program and portfolio offices have many similar functions, but each has a different focus. There needs to be close cooperation between them, but this does not necessarily mean that they must be located in the same physical area. They can be combined or separate, they may be in the same or different locations, there may be multiple project offices, there may even be multiple program offices but there will usually only be one portfolio office.

The following diagram illustrates the position of the portfolio office within the portfolio management structure (titles may vary from organization to organization):

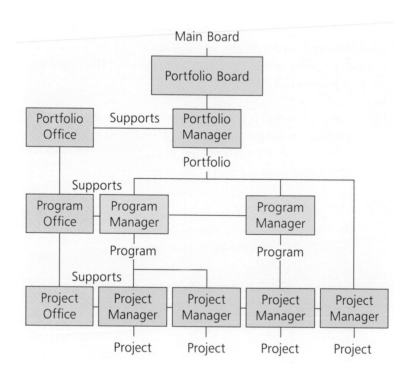

Hot tip

This diagram illustrates a simplistic structure, where project managers report to program managers who, in turn, report to the portfolio manager. In practice there may be other reporting chains through project and program boards.

The responsibilities of the portfolio office are broadly similar to those of the program office but they have a slightly different focus. While a program office is chiefly concerned with tracking project progress against time, cost and ultimately benefit realization, the portfolio office is solely concerned with tracking the value of the delivered products.

Governance

For many organizations, managing projects has always been something of a challenge. While it is obviously critical to a business that they are managed effectively, research has shown that the majority of organizations fail in this respect. Studies of IT projects in particular have shown that only around 30 percent of projects are successful, while the remainder either fail totally or fail to deliver the expected benefits. Proper portfolio governance ensures that projects are prioritized on a business benefit basis and monitored throughout their life cycle.

Integrating Governance

The governance mechanisms in a portfolio are most effective when integrated with the corporate governance already used in an organization. Portfolio governance tightly integrated with corporate governance will ensure that the investment in projects creates real value for the business. Governance is the responsibility of the top executives or board of directors and consists of the leadership, organizational structures and processes that ensure that the enterprise's strategies and objectives are delivered through the selected projects.

Governance is the control framework through which portfolios deliver their change objectives and remain within corporate visibility and control. The whole purpose of grouping projects into a portfolio is to ensure governance of the portfolio at the highest level in the organization.

Governance is about structured decision making on investments in projects as has been summarized as the four 'ares':

- Are we doing the right projects?

- Are we doing them the right way?

- Are we getting them done well?

- Are we getting the benefits?

Most project management methodologies focus on the delivery aspect of projects (doing them the right way), but very little on strategic alignment or value. What is needed is a framework that addresses the entire life cycle of a project and its product. Portfolio management ensures that the right projects are chosen and that the business benefits are captured.

Portfolio Organization

The following diagram illustrates a typical portfolio management organization. The portfolio board reports to the main board.

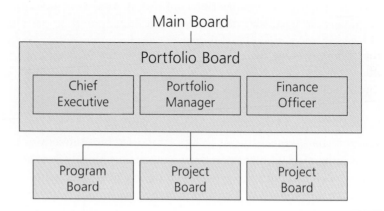

Main Board

The main board or executive group are the organization's top management. They are accountable for operational as well as business change governance. Their role is to ensure that the organization's business strategies, mission and vision are achieved through its change initiatives.

Portfolio Board

The portfolio board (or steering group) is responsible for selecting the portfolio, realizing the benefits, stakeholder engagement and information management. It will typically consists of the chief executive officer (CEO), chief financial officer (CFO) and the portfolio manager, together with any other required skills (such as portfolio office) or stakeholder representation.

The CEO heads the portfolio board and takes ultimate accountability for the achievement of the enterprise's portfolio of projects. The CFO performs the role of investment adviser to the portfolio board. The portfolio manager (who may also be a member of the main board) manages the portfolio assisted by the portfolio office.

The portfolio board may have responsibility for change control and investment review or there may be separate change control and investment review boards.

The portfolio board will be appointed by the main board and charged with selecting and managing the portfolio. The portfolio will consist of a number of programs and projects and the relevant program and project boards will report in to the portfolio board.

Portfolio Definition

The portfolio manager will, with the assistance of the portfolio office, identify all the known and potential programs, projects and other change initiatives within the organization. These will then be evaluated against the organization's strategy and vision and rated as set out in portfolio selection (pages 64-65) for review by the portfolio board. Once agreed, the portfolio manager will then develop the portfolio strategy and delivery plan for review and authorization by the board.

The portfolio definition process should be repeated at regular time intervals (three to six months) to include newly identified projects and potentially remove redundant projects from the portfolio.

Portfolio Delivery

Again, with the assistance of the portfolio office, the portfolio manager will carry out the organizational governance role by carrying out the benefits realization management, portfolio risk management and stakeholder management functions.

During the portfolio delivery phase, the portfolio board will be monitoring and accepting progress reports from the programs and projects in the portfolio. Identified risks and issues may be escalated to the board for consideration and overall benefits realization will be monitored.

Capability Delivery

Individual programs and projects within the portfolio deliver the capability that will enable the realization of benefits. The responsible project and program boards are accountable for the success of their projects and delivery of the required capability. They are also responsible for effective reporting on progress.

Operational Management

The final piece of the portfolio organization is the operational line management, who are responsible for putting the new capability into production (business as usual) and actual realization of the business benefits.

Beware

Without the active cooperation and support of operational management, even the best business change initiatives can fail.

133

Key Processes

In addition to the precursors listed earlier in this chapter, there are a further nine key process areas that will need to be implemented to support effective portfolio management:

1 **Transition Management:** to ensure that the relevant business areas are ready and prepared for the implementation of project outputs. Transition plans should be produced to reflect the activities required to ensure that the business environment is ready to exploit the new capability, when delivered, and address any implications for the ongoing business operations

2 **Information Management:** to maximize the efficiency with which the organization plans, collects, organizes, utilizes, controls, disseminates and finally disposes of information. It should ensure that the potential value of information is identified and exploited to support internal business operations and add value to service delivery

3 **Organizational Focus:** to establish the leadership and necessary responsibility for program and project management activities with the aim of improving the organization's overall capability. The program and project management activities should be standardized and fully integrated into the business processes

4 **Process Definition:** to develop and maintain a set of program and project management process assets that can be used by all programs and projects to improve performance and provide cumulative benefits to the organization. These assets should include the definition of the organization's standard program and project management processes, life cycle descriptions, templates, guidelines and supporting documentation libraries

5 **Competency Development:** to develop the skills and knowledge (supplemented with coaching and mentoring) of program and project managers, their teams and any other personnel engaged with programs and projects, so they can perform their roles more effectively

6. **Integrated Management and Reporting:** to ensure that all program and project activities (including management and administration) form a coherent set, developed from the organization's standard approach and related process assets. Integrated management necessitates the development of program and project plans that address the specific outcomes being sought by the business. Plans should be based on defined processes and describe how the activities will be implemented and managed. The emphasis of integrated management is to anticipate problems and other issues and to act to prevent or minimize the effects of these problems

7. **Life Cycle Control:** to ensure the consistent performance of program and project activities in terms of well-defined process and to produce consistent deliverables and other outputs effectively and efficiently. Life cycle control ensures that the necessary activities to design, build and maintain the desired outputs are accomplished using appropriate tools and methods, and that the process of transformation is conducted economically and value can be demonstrated

8. **Inter Group Coordination:** to establish the means for teams to communicate and actively engage with other teams in order to satisfy more adequately the business and customer needs in an efficient and effective manner

9. **Quality Assurance:** to provide organizational assurance that programs and projects have suitable quality plans and measures to ensure that their processes are suitably controlled and are likely to result in deliverables that meet explicit quality criteria. Quality assurance augments quality control in ensuring that quality is planned into all programs and projects, rather than relying on inspection and removal of defects in deliverables

While these key processes all relate to project and program management maturity, they are nevertheless required in order to support portfolio management.

Implementation

The introduction and implementation of portfolio management in an organization is a significant change in itself and should be treated as a project (or possibly even a program) in its own right. There are a number of topics that will need to be addressed, starting with the culture of the organization.

Top Management

Effective implementation of portfolio management will require the backing and commitment of the top management of the organization. This means executive or board-level sponsorship with full visibility and engagement with program and project boards and any other involved parties.

Organizational Competence

Knowledge and awareness of portfolio management is required across the entire organization, not just in the project and program management community. All disciplines and functions should be engaged and committed. Operations managers need to be aware of program and project management procedures to enable them to contribute effectively to the outcomes of change projects as they are implemented.

Specialist Roles

In addition to top management's role, there are a number of specialist roles that can prove valuable in supporting the adoption of portfolio management:

- Portfolio management champions in each business area who will promote portfolio management awareness

- Including some elements of portfolio management in staff job descriptions will also help to develop their awareness

- Include change delivery objectives for key line management staff with links to the achievement of benefits

- Give suitable levels of authority to those in portfolio management positions

In addition to the standard roles within a portfolio structure, there may also be benefit in defining roles for nominated individuals in areas such as:

- Risk and issue management

- Benefits management

- Planning

- Communications

- Quality management

- Change and configuration control

Implementation Process

A key part of the implementation process is the staff training, education and awareness. This needs to be supported by documented processes, procedures, standards and guidelines. The following should form the outline for an implementation plan:

1. Ensure the organizational maturity and portfolio office are developed, set up and ready

2. Document a standard approach, processes and methods for running a portfolio, which cover the key process areas

3. Gain top organizational commitment to use these processes and methods

4. Develop tools and templates, which will enable consistency and will drive best practice within the business, while avoiding the creation of unnecessary bureaucracy

5. Produce a training program to ensure all relevant staff are familiar with the approach, processes, methods, tools and templates

6. Ensure that quality assurance activities are built into the portfolio office to maintain a focus on process efficiency and improvement

Once this is all in place, the organization is ready to start up and run a portfolio. This is covered in the next chapter, Managing a Portfolio.

Summary

- Portfolio management can be implemented with or without the implementation of program management and it will bring significant benefits to the organization

- To implement portfolio management there must be a basic level of organizational maturity in place covering project (and program if relevant) management

- Unless the organization is fairly small it will also be beneficial to establish a portfolio office to provide support to the portfolio manager

- Portfolio governance should be tightly integrated with organizational governance and is all about selecting the best projects in line with organizational strategy

- Other precursors that need to be in place are: organizational vision statement, stakeholder engagement policy, benefits management, planning and control, business case, risk and issue management and senior management commitment

- The portfolio organization should consist of a portfolio board or steering group consisting of at least the CEO, CFO (or other financial adviser) and the portfolio manager

- During portfolio definition the projects and programs will be evaluated and prioritized, during portfolio delivery the benefits realization will be tracked

- There are nine key process areas that should be implemented to support portfolio management: transition management, information management, organizational focus, process definition, competency development, integrated management and reporting, life cycle control, inter-group coordination and quality assurance

- The implementation of portfolio management in an organization is a significant change and should be treated as a project (or possibly program) in its own right

- Implementation of portfolio management requires top management commitment and involvement, documentation of the portfolio management processes, tools and templates and training for portfolio staff

9 Managing a Portfolio

This chapter examines what is involved in managing a portfolio through the definition and delivery phases.

Introduction

We looked at the portfolio life cycle in Chapter 4 and defined the two phases, two drivers and six processes as illustrated below:

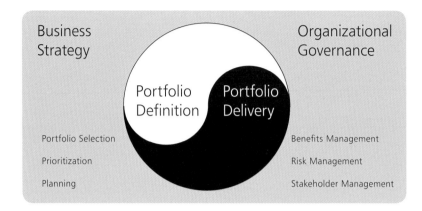

In this chapter we will be looking in more depth at what is involved in managing these phases and processes:

Preparation

Before portfolio definition can begin there are a number of preparatory steps that need to be carried out, starting with the 10 essential prerequisites and some key processes (pages 142 to 143). The portfolio manager and portfolio board need to be appointed and the portfolio manager will need to start defining and documenting the portfolio management processes.

Portfolio Definition

The portfolio definition phase is driven by the business strategy and during this phase the portfolio manager should be asking two of the four 'are' questions: "Are we doing the right things?" and "Are we doing them in the right way?" The definition phase consists of three main processes:

1 **Portfolio Selection:** first, all of the change initiatives (potential and existing projects and programs) should be reviewed and those that map onto the organization's business strategy should be selected for potential inclusion in the portfolio (this is covered on pages 144 to 145)

2 **Portfolio Prioritization:** next, the selected change initiatives should be ranked based on appropriate metrics and the portfolio is then balanced based on available resources, funding, contribution to objectives, business impact and risk (covered on pages 146 to 147)

3 **Portfolio Plan:** once approved by the portfolio board, the portfolio information should then be collated to create the portfolio strategy and portfolio delivery plan for authorization by the portfolio board (pages 148 to 149)

Following the approval of the plan, the portfolio moves onto the portfolio delivery phase. However, the definition phase is repeated at regular intervals (typically every three to six months) to keep the portfolio in line with the business strategy and emerging market opportunities.

Portfolio Delivery

The portfolio delivery phase is driven by the organizational governance and during this phase the portfolio manager should be asking the other two of the four 'are' questions: "Are we doing them well?" and "Are we getting the benefits?" Again, the delivery phase consists of three main processes:

1 **Benefits Management:** the realization of benefits is delivered through the programs and projects that make up the portfolio, but they do not on their own produce benefits, they enable the realization of benefits through the change initiatives they deliver (pages 150 to 151)

2 **Risk Management:** each of the components of the portfolio should be evaluated for risks (and opportunities), together with the cost impact of the risk resolution and how these risks may impact on the achievement of the strategic plan and objectives (pages 152 to 153)

3 **Stakeholder Management:** to ensure that the needs of all stakeholders are identified and managed accordingly through effective communication (pages 154 to 155)

As the portfolio management cycle is continuous and reiterative it is constantly repeated from each review of the portfolio.

Preparation

Before the portfolio selection process can begin there are a number of precursors that need to be in place. These were documented in detail in Chapter 8 but in summary they are:

1 **Organizational Maturity:** portfolio management will not work unless the organization has established maturity in its project management methodology. It must be at least at project management maturity level three (defined) with centrally controlled processes documented and in place together with an awareness of what a program and portfolio of projects are

2 **Portfolio Office:** unless the organization is a small one and the portfolio manager is going to carry out all the functions of a portfolio office, it will be necessary to establish a portfolio office. Most organizations at a project management maturity level three will already have a project office in place and the portfolio office can be developed from this (see page 130)

3 **Governance:** portfolio management will not be effective unless there is a good culture and understanding of project governance in place in the organization. Portfolio governance is based on and totally dependent on good project governance

4 **Portfolio Organization:** the portfolio board is a prerequisite for portfolio management as all the key decisions on the portfolio emanate from the board. If no portfolio board has been appointed, the responsibility will fall to the main board

5 **Business Strategy:** portfolio selection is driven by and must map onto the organization's strategic business objectives. These, therefore, need to be established and in place based on the organization's mission and vision statements

6 **Benefits Management:** there must be standards and processes in place for the definition, calculation and realization of benefits for every project. This is an essential part of the portfolio management process both in the selection and realization processes

7 **Risk and Issue Management:** processes and standards must be defined for the identification, management, mitigation and reporting of portfolio risks and issues

8 **Stakeholder Management:** again this is essential for portfolio management to work so there must be an existing culture of stakeholder engagement with documented policy and processes

9 **Planning and Control:** processes and standards must exist for planning and control as these are key elements in portfolio management

10 **Senior Management Commitment:** without a high level of top management commitment, understanding and active participation in portfolio management, it will fail

These 10 precursors are essential for portfolio management to work. If they are not already established they will need to be implemented before the portfolio selection process starts.

Key Processes

In addition to the precursors listed above, there were nine key processes listed and described (on pages 134 to 135). These are: transition management, information management, organizational focus, process definition, competency development, integrated management and reporting, life cycle control, inter group coordination and quality assurance. While these are not as critical as the precursors, if they are not currently in place they should be introduced as soon as possible in the portfolio life cycle.

Portfolio Start Up

Portfolio start up begins with the appointment of the portfolio manager and portfolio board. Once appointed, the portfolio manager will need to begin the portfolio selection process in conjunction with the portfolio board.

Don't forget

The portfolio manager will also need to begin defining the portfolio management standards and methodology in conjunction with the portfolio office.

Selection

The portfolio selection process really starts with making sure there is a clear corporate strategy in place that can be used for selecting and prioritizing change initiatives. The selection process then begins with these four steps:

1 The organization's corporate vision statement must be expressed in terms of business direction (where the organization wishes to be in future)

2 The business direction then needs to be expressed in terms of a working strategy (how the business is going to get there)

3 The working strategy then needs to be stated as a number of specific objectives (things that can be achieved over a specific time frame)

4 Finally, achieving the specific objectives will require change initiatives (projects or programs)

Each of the change initiatives must be defined in some form but it is generally not developed to the level of a project brief or program mandate (it precedes these in a portfolio managed environment). It should include outline objectives, business benefits, cost and the risks. In addition to new change initiatives there will almost certainly be ongoing projects in the organization and these also need to be included in the selection process in the same way. These proposed and active change initiatives then form the raw input to the selection process.

Project Database

The portfolio management process will require a central project database to record the summary details of all existing and proposed projects in the organization for selection, evaluation and reporting purposes. This is generally populated as part of the business planning process and should be updated periodically (such as quarterly) in order to assess potential new programs and projects against the existing portfolio.

When developing the initial ratings of projects and programs it is advisable to use clear metrics to remove any subjectivity from the

Hot tip

The project database does not need to be a sophisticated database; a spreadsheet will usually suffice to start with.

process. It is also necessary to review and refine the ratings and metrics periodically to ensure they remain relevant.

Stakeholder Engagement

The information used to populate the database should not be developed by the portfolio office in isolation. Key stakeholders should be involved to build consensus on the content.

The actual selection and rating process should involve senior stakeholders from all the relevant parts of the organization. This could be a formal selection committee, a series of facilitated workshops, or just a series of meetings but it is vital to involve all the interested parties.

Rating Process

Each change initiative needs to be rated against an agreed set of criteria and metrics. These could include:

- The type of initiative: new business opportunity, operational efficiency, regulatory requirement, etc.

- Alignment with corporate strategy and objectives

- Cost/benefit analysis and cash flow impact

- Level of effort required (low/medium/high)

- Project or corporate risk

Ratings can be on a simple high/medium/low basis or a more detailed numerical scale. One simple way of achieving a primary ranking is to rate each project's alignment to corporate strategy by assessing whether it is strategic (contributes to corporate goals), efficiency (increase output or reduce costs) or operational (to maintain services). Then ranking it by the amount of effort required to implement it.

MuSCoW Ratings

The projects can then be ranked as: Must have (strategic low effort projects), Should have (efficiency or operational low effort projects), Could have (strategic high effort projects) or Won't have (efficiency or operational high effort projects).

The portfolio is now ready to move onto the next stage of prioritization and optimization.

Prioritization

Once the portfolio has been selected and given some sort of preliminary ranking, it can be shared with the key stakeholders to validate and refine where necessary. At this stage the portfolio only provides decision support information to assist the portfolio board in prioritizing the programs and projects that are best aligned to strategic drivers, with the least risk to the organization.

Prioritization

The prioritization process takes the list of potential programs and projects and assesses each to identify the optimum portfolio. This also has to take account of organizational constraints such as availability of investment funds and human resources.

Project Request

To enable prioritization to occur, it is necessary to collect some initial information about a program or project proposal. This is best done by using some form of project and program request form, which will allow:

- The business operations to register an idea with the portfolio office for investment evaluation and to make a potential funding decision

- The portfolio office to collect enough information to be able to evaluate the proposal in a prioritization model before significant work commences

This form can also be used as the entry point to an investment gateway review process (covered in Chapter 10), which assesses the ongoing viability of a project or program at key points of its life cycle and into benefits realization.

The prioritization process assesses two components of each potential program or project:

- The proposed change initiative itself, how well it is aligned to strategy, the cost and potential return on investment

- The delivery and execution capability of the organization to be able to manage, deliver and implement it

Other factors that should be considered in the prioritization process are the type of project, resource availability (or limitations) and the need to maximize the total portfolio benefit.

Some organizations use a 'hurdle rate' or minimum return on investment (ROI) rate to ensure that projects return a positive benefit.

Assessment

The final assessment of each project or program could be carried out using the following types of evaluation criteria:

1 **Project Type:** is it mandatory (to meet regulatory or operational continuity requirements) or discretionary (to meet business needs, increase efficiency or infrastructure)?

2 **Strategic Fit:** is it critical, important, supportive (one or more strategic priorities), tenuous or has no link?

3 **Potential Benefit:** the expected net present value of the business benefits (which is likely to be a range rather than an exact figure)

4 **Cost:** the expected net present cost of the project (which is also likely to be a range rather than an exact figure)

5 **Non Quantifiable Benefits:** any other benefits such as customer satisfaction or business simplification

6 **Resources:** are the resources required to deliver the project fully available, partly available or not available?

7 **Delivery Risk:** is it a high, medium or low risk and high, medium or low complexity?

An agreed weighting should be given to each criterion and the knowledge and experience of the portfolio board is then used to select the best possible mix of projects for the portfolio.

Balancing

The final step is to balance the portfolio by adding or removing projects in order to achieve the best possible outcome for the organization with the human resources and finance available to it.

This may require several iterations before the board is satisfied with the portfolio. It must then be communicated to all the key stakeholders for final feedback and comment and then authorized by the portfolio board and main board if necessary.

Hot tip

Some initiatives may be included conditionally and it is important to capture the conditions under which they were included.

Planning

Once the prioritized portfolio has been agreed by the portfolio board and authorized by the main board the portfolio information can be collated to create the portfolio strategy and portfolio delivery plan.

Portfolio Strategy

The portfolio strategy explains how the portfolio meets the organization's strategic objectives. The portfolio strategy can also be used to develop a portfolio charter. The portfolio strategy should consist of:

Hot tip

All of these factors will change over time, so a snapshot should be captured every time the portfolio is revised.

1 A list of each of the component projects in the portfolio, mapped to one or more of the strategic objectives and a description how they support the attainment of the objective or objectives

2 A description of how the available finance and human resources have been allocated to meet the strategic objectives

3 An explanation of how the selection, prioritization, balancing and termination of portfolio components will be managed to ensure continuing alignment with changing strategic goals and organizational priorities

Delivery Plan

The delivery plan will need to cover the period of time from the start of the first project to the end of delivery for the last project in the portfolio. Each of the component projects and programs should be examined and assessed for suitability. It might be more appropriate to treat a large project as a program. Project inter-relationships should be examined to determine if there is any case for treating a group of projects as a program. Finally, stand-alone projects should be considered for potential inclusion in any of the existing programs. The delivery plan should cover the following:

1 **Road Map:** should set out how and when the individual components will be executed and their inter-relationships

2 **Management Plan:** this should set out exactly how governance will be exercised over the portfolio. It should define what infrastructure and systems will be used to support the portfolio management process. It should explain how the portfolio will be reviewed, re-prioritized and optimized to ensure continuing alignment with evolving organizational goals and opportunities. It should also explain how legal and regulatory requirements will be met. Finally, it should set out how participation in project and program reviews will be used to reflect senior level support, leadership and involvement in key decisions

3 **Performance Management:** this should state how component performance will be measured, how the value will be determined, how financial management will be performed and how the supply of and demand for resources will be managed. It should describe how the value to the organization will be measured and monitored and how triggers for any authorized tolerances will be set and monitored

4 **Communication Management:** which should set out how the timely and appropriate generation, collection, distribution, storage, retrieval and ultimately disposal of portfolio information will be carried out. It should describe how key stakeholders will be provided with timely information on portfolio component selection, prioritization and performance as well as early notification of and involvement in portfolio level risks and issues that may impact performance

5 **Risk Management:** should define how portfolio risks will be managed through the processes of identification, analysis, response planning, monitoring and controlling

6 **Portfolio Office:** the role of the portfolio office and its interaction with the portfolio manager, portfolio board and the component projects and programs. It should also describe how these portfolio management processes will be established and maintained together with a supporting framework (conceptual and communicable structure of ideas) and methodology (policies and procedures)

Benefits Management

The benefits management process begins with establishing the business value of any change initiative.

Business Value
The definition of business value will vary from one organization to another but, in general, it refers to the entire value of the business based on its tangible and intangible assets. Business benefits are therefore anything that can add to this business value.

The projected business benefits from any change establishes the business case (justification) for carrying out the required project or program. In a portfolio environment these benefits need to be aligned to the organization's strategic objectives.

Benefits Delivery
The actual realization of the benefits is delivered through the programs and projects that make up the portfolio. But the programs and projects will rarely produce these benefits on their own, rather they enable the realization of benefits through the change initiatives that they deliver.

The actual benefits are realized by the operational management responsible for the ongoing changed business processes. However, the portfolio manager's involvement begins with the initiation of the projects or programs that make up the portfolio.

Project Initiation
The inclusion of any project in a portfolio is based on two key factors:

- The projected benefits that the project will deliver

- The organization's ability to execute the project in a timely and competent manner

However, at the portfolio definition phase, there are only preliminary estimates available, so all projects need to go through a start up and initiation process. This should result in a project charter, business case and project plan together with the appointment of a project manager and project board.

The portfolio manager must be involved in the authorization and approval of these key documents and gives authorization for the project to begin provided that the business benefits are still in line with or improve on the initial projection. If this is not the case, then potentially the project can be removed from the portfolio.

Project Governance

During the execution phase of a project the portfolio manager is concerned with the delivery of the required capabilities and organizational change required to leverage those capabilities. They will need to receive regular progress reports from each project or program so that they can track progress and costs in order to ensure that each component is still on track to deliver the projected benefits.

They will need to provide any advice, guidance and support needed by the project or program managers. They will need to provide any tools and techniques that the project managers may need to optimize their performance. They will also need to maximize the effectiveness of resources between projects in order to provide the necessary capacity and skills.

Project Implementation

As a project moves towards its implementation stage the portfolio manager will need to ensure that the business organization is gearing up ready to make the most of the delivered capability and begin to realize the benefits.

Benefits Measurement

In order to be able to measure benefits realization effectively, it is essential that all existing measurements are taken and recorded as a benchmark. The portfolio manager will need to ensure that the operational management have accepted full responsibility for the benefits realization process and have put the required benefits reporting procedures in place.

Benefits Reporting

Benefits often start to accrue gradually at first. First of all there is a new system or process for people to become familiar with. Then there may be a period of parallel running while both systems or processes are used until such time as there is a full cut over to the new procedures. As a result, benefits realization normally ramps up and this needs to be reflected in the benefits reporting. Benefits measurement and reporting need to be continued until a firm set of figures for the results of each change initiative have been established and can be compared to the projected benefits.

At the portfolio level, risks can be thought of as chances that can have good or bad outcomes, hence opportunities.

Risk Management

Each of the component programs and projects of the portfolio should be evaluated for risks (and opportunities) at the organizational level in the light of how these risks may impact on the achievement of the strategic plan and objectives. The risks that need to be tracked and monitored are the project risks, inter-project risks and organizational or business risks. Whatever type of risk they are, there should be a standard approach to dealing with them:

Risk Identification

Project risks should be identified at the project level and reported up to the portfolio manager as part of regular reporting procedures. Inter project risks could come from one or more of the projects in the portfolio or they may be identified by the portfolio manager or portfolio office. Business risks are more likely to be identified by the portfolio board or main board. These are risks such as market changes and legislative changes.

Wherever the risks come from, they must be recorded in the portfolio risk log so they can be tracked.

Risk Estimation

Each identified risk needs to be estimated for its probability (how likely it is to occur) and its impact (what will happen if it does occur) on the project. Project risks should be reported with these two factors estimated but at the portfolio level, it is the potential impact on the portfolio that is of more concern and that may be different from the impact on the project.

These details should then be added to the risk log.

Risk Evaluation

Having rated the probability and potential impact of each risk it can then be evaluated against a probability impact grid (as illustrated at the top of the page opposite):

1. All high probability/high impact risks need to be addressed as the top priority, as not only are they very likely to occur but they are also likely to have a significant impact on the portfolio

2. Next, any high/medium and medium/high risks need to be addressed as the second priority

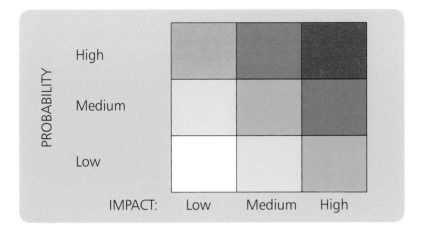

3 Then high/low and medium/medium risks can be considered with less urgency and so on

Risk Countermeasures

As each risk is considered there are five main options for dealing with the risk:

● **Prevention:** which will usually be an expensive option

● **Reduction:** of either the probability and/or impact

● **Acceptance:** if the cost of prevention or reduction would be prohibitive or it is worth taking the risk

● **Transfer:** the risk is transferred to a third party such as a supplier or an insurance provider

● **Contingency planning:** to prepare in advance what will need to be done if and when the risk occurs

One or more of these options should be selected for each risk and the details added to the risk log.

Monitoring and Controlling

Once the countermeasures have been planned, resourced and put into place the risks need to be monitored on an ongoing basis. If a risk does occur then any contingency plan can be brought into play or other actions taken as appropriate. Over time, risks will change and this should be reflected in the risk log.

Beware

All contingency budgets should be allocated to individual risks so they cannot be used for general project overrun.

153

Stakeholder Management

Stakeholder management is carried out to ensure that the needs of all portfolio stakeholders are identified and managed accordingly through effective communications. Program stakeholder management was described in Chapter 3 (pages 46 to 47) and portfolio stakeholder management is broadly similar.

Stakeholder Engagement

The portfolio manager needs to be in frequent contact with the portfolio stakeholders and should also encourage communication between stakeholders to gain common agreement and enable better portfolio decisions to be made. The key to effective portfolio stakeholder management is the development of a portfolio communications management plan:

Don't forget

Special care needs to be taken when dealing with and planning for engagement with negative stakeholders.

1 Identify all the portfolio stakeholders (as described on page 46)

2 Identify their expectations for the portfolio and any special needs for information or other involvement they might have (this is always best accomplished through face-to-face meetings)

3 Develop this information into a list of communications requirements and identify how each is best addressed (regular reports, meetings, dashboards and so on)

4 This then forms the draft portfolio communications management plan, which can be taken back to the stakeholders to confirm their needs and the proposed ways of addressing them

Having produced and agreed the portfolio communications management plan, it should become the driver for stakeholder communication. However, people's needs will change over time so it is essential to keep the communications management plan up-to-date to reflect these changed needs.

Change Management

Another area of stakeholder management is change management. It is the very nature of a portfolio that it will change as the business changes and new opportunities present themselves.

However, adding new projects to a portfolio and removing ones that are no longer strategic to the business can have a significant impact on stakeholders.

Change can happen for a variety of reasons: a new business opportunity, a new legal requirement, new technology has become available or someone has just thought of a better way to do something. Whatever the reason, change needs to be handled in a controlled way:

1 Work out what the implications of the change to the portfolio will be (if additional work will have to be done, if anything will no longer be required or if any completed projects will need to be changed)

2 Identify which stakeholders are impacted by these changes to the portfolio and what the implications are likely to be (and whether they will see the changes as a good thing or a bad thing)

3 Meet with the impacted stakeholders (either individually or as a group) to go through the proposed changes and the reasons for them

4 Try to obtain their agreement to the proposed changes or at the very least their understanding for why the changes are required

5 Document everything so all stakeholders will have a copy and will understand what is happening

One group of stakeholders who may well be impacted in a negative way are any project managers and project team members on projects which are going to be frozen or canceled as a result of a change. These will require delicate handling.

The portfolio manager needs to be able to deal with all stakeholders in an appropriate and understanding way, whether they are senior management or more junior employees. Providing the portfolio strategy (page 148) is sound, stakeholders should at least understand (if not agree with) the reason for the change.

Summary

- The portfolio life cycle consists of two phases (portfolio definition and portfolio delivery), two drivers (business strategy and organizational governance) and six processes (portfolio selection, portfolio prioritization, portfolio plan, benefits management, risk management and stakeholder management)

- Before the first process (portfolio selection) can begin there are a number of precursors that need to be in place including: organizational maturity, portfolio office, governance, business strategy and senior management commitment

- Portfolio selection starts from the organization's vision statement, producing the business direction, working strategy, specific objectives and then mapping the necessary change initiatives (projects and programs) to those objectives

- Each change initiative then needs to be rated with the involvement of the key stakeholders

- The proposed portfolio then needs to be prioritized to reflect how well each component is aligned to corporate strategy and how able the organization will be able to deliver and implement it. Once this is done it can be balanced to achieve the best possible outcome with the finance and resources available

- The portfolio strategy and delivery plan are then drawn up from the available data to illustrate how the portfolio will be executed and managed

- Benefits management takes place through the definition of benefits, project initiation, project governance, implementation and benefits measurement and reporting

- Portfolio risk management should be a documented process that covers risk identification, risk estimation, risk evaluation, countermeasures and ongoing monitoring and controlling

- Stakeholder management should be planned and executed through stakeholder engagement, communications and change management

10 Gateway Reviews

This chapter explains the gateway review process and how it can be applied to large projects and programs for improved governance.

Introduction

Following a string of high profile project failures in the UK, the Office of Government Commerce (OGC) introduced a gateway review process in 2001. The process consists of a series of short peer reviews at key stages of a project or program. The reviews are intended to highlight risks and issues which, if not addressed, could threaten the success of the project or program.

The concept of gateway reviews has subsequently been taken up and developed by many other organizations worldwide. The process can be applied to all types of projects and programs, but is most effective when applied to larger projects and programs.

Gateway Reviews

The peer reviews should be carried out by an independent team of experienced people, selected for their relevant skills (for a small organization this could be external consultants). UK government reviews require reviewers to complete a training and accreditation process, but this is not essential in a normal business environment.

Reviews typically take between one and four days and are usually carried out by a team of around three people. But the team could be larger or smaller depending on the complexity of the project or program under review and the range of skills and expertise it spans. On completion of the review, the review team will normally discuss their initial findings with the project or program's senior responsible owner (SRO) before issuing their final report giving their assessment and recommendations.

Project Review

Project reviews examine a project at five key stages in its life cycle and consider its readiness to progress to the next stage. The five review gateways are:

Full gateway reviews would be inappropriate for smaller projects. However, a mini gateway review (to cover a subset of the key topics) could be used if required.

The project review gateways are illustrated relative to the project life cycle on page 161.

1. **Business Justification:** gateway one confirms that the business case is sound, it meets the needs of the business and is affordable and achievable

2. **Delivery Strategy:** gateway two confirms that the business case is still sound based on the proposed delivery strategy, the delivery approach is appropriate, the delivery plan is realistic, project and financial controls are in place and that human and financial resources are available

3   **Investment Decision:** gateway three confirms that the business case (including the benefits management plan) is still sound and aligned with the organization's business strategy (or program to which it contributes) and is likely to deliver the specified outcomes on time, within budget and will provide value-for-money

4   **Readiness for Service:** gateway four confirms that an implementation plan has been developed in line with the organization's policies and industry best practice; that the solution provided is fit for purpose, affordable and any risks have been identified; that the business case remains valid and the projected benefits are likely to be achieved

5   **Benefits Evaluation:** gateway five assesses whether the business case for the project was realistic and is still valid; that the anticipated benefits are being delivered and lessons learned have been captured and are being shared within the organization

Program Review

In addition to the five project gateways, if the projects form part of a program there will also be a program gateway (gateway zero):

1   **Strategic Assessment:** gateway zero review is carried out at various stages in a program to: check the outcomes and objectives for the program and confirm it makes the necessary contribution to the overall strategy of the organization; ensure users and key stakeholders support the program; review the arrangements for leading and managing the program and its individual projects; review the means of identifying and managing program risks; ensure financial and human resources are provided; and ensure plans for the existing and next stage are realistic

The gateway review process provides support to SROs to ensure that: the best available skills and experience are deployed on the program or project; all stakeholders understand the current status and any issues; the program or project can progress to the next stage; and the projected benefits will be realized.

Gateway five can be performed multiple times, if necessary, during benefits realization and before final decommissioning of the project output.

The program review gateways are illustrated relative to the program life cycle on page 160.

159

Program Overview

Don't forget

The delivery cycle is repeated for each project in the program and there can be multiple assessments during this phase.

Program

Definition

Preparation

Initiation

Gateway 0: First Strategic Assessment

Delivery

Planning

Execution

Benefits Realization

Gateway 0: Middle Stage Assessments

Closure

Close Out

Transition

Gateway 0: Final Strategic Assessment

Project Overview

Projects

Initiation
Strategy
Analysis
Design & Build
Implementation
Operational Service
Decommission

Gateway 1:
Business Justification

Gateway 2:
Delivery Strategy

Gateway 3:
Investment Decision

Gateway 4:
Readiness for Service

Gateway 5:
Benefits Realization

Hot tip

In this example you might also want to repeat the gateway 3 review following the design and before starting the build.

Don't forget

Gateway five can be performed multiple times, if necessary, during benefits realization and before final decommissioning of the project output.

Strategic Investment

Gateway 0: the strategic investment is a review of the program either at the end of a phase to ratify that it is ready to move onto the next phase or during the delivery phase to review the overall progress of the program. The purpose of the review is to:

Gateway 0 is only applicable to programs and not to individual stand alone projects.

- Review the objectives of the program and confirm that they (still) contribute to the strategy of the organization

- Ensure the business case for the program is (still) sound and that the program is affordable

- Ensure the key stakeholders understand the scope of the program and (still) support it

- Confirm that the program's potential to succeed has been considered in the context of the organization's delivery plans and other programs and projects

- Review the arrangements for program governance and in particular the links to constituent projects

- Review the arrangements for identifying and managing program and project risks (including external risks)

- Ensure adequate human and financial resources are provided

- Ensure plans for the current and next phase are realistic and properly resourced, including the constituent projects

In addition to the above, after the initial program review:

- Review actual progress to date against plans, expected outcomes, the business case and benefits management plan

- Confirm the planned outcomes are still achievable, any changes in scope or value have been properly agreed and the business case has been reviewed and revised if necessary

- Ensure the key stakeholders are still confident that outcomes will be achieved when expected

- Confirm that the major risks have been identified and risk management plans are in place for them together with contingency plans and a business continuity plan

- Check if lessons from similar programs have been considered

A set of checklists for gateway reviews zero to five are available on our website. Go to www.ineasysteps. com/resource-centre/ downloads/

When the program is ready to move on to the next phase:

- Confirm that funds are available to continue the program and that it is still affordable

- Confirm that the required human resources are available, suitably skilled and committed to undertake the work

- Confirm that the plans to progress the program are realistic and achievable

- Confirm that appropriate management controls are in place

- Confirm that the business case is established and is being maintained to keep it up-to-date

- Confirm that a benefit management plan is active and that benefits are being tracked and reported

The Review

Around six to eight weeks before the review, the dates and people required for the review team should be established. The program team should provide the review team with as much documentation as possible and identify the most appropriate stakeholders to interview. The scope of the review should be established, with any special areas of concern.

At the end of the review, the review team will present the SRO with its findings and recommendations. The report should give the program an overall status rating together with status ratings for each of the individual recommendations. These are given a red, amber or green (RAG) status, depending on the importance of the recommendation or overall status of the project as follows:

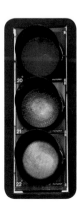

Red (critical and urgent): immediate action needs to be taken on the recommendations or the project or program is likely to fail.

Amber (critical but not urgent): the program can move ahead but action on the recommendations should be addressed before key decisions are taken.

Green: the program is on target to succeed but may benefit from the uptake of recommendations.

Benefits Justification

Gateway 1: benefits justification is the first review of a stand alone project or a constituent project of a program. The purpose of the review is to confirm that the business case is sound, meets the business needs, is affordable and achievable and is likely to achieve value for money. It also confirms that the project is ready to move ahead to the next stage.

Business Case

The key document in the review is the business case. This sets out the justification for the project. If the project is part of a program it may not produce financial benefits in its own right but may be an enabling project. This should still be quantified and documented in the business case. The review should:

- Confirm that the business case is complete and consistent with organizational standards and guidelines

- Establish that there is a clear and agreed understanding of the business objectives and how they will be delivered, together with any essential activities that must be performed if the objectives of the project are to be achieved

- Confirm that critical success factors are documented together with how they will be measured or quantified

- Establish that the business case has examined a wide range of options for solution and delivery of the business needs

- Establish that the whole-life costs and benefits were analyzed for all options

- Confirm if there is one clear best option, or if several options could meet the business needs

- If there are several options, confirm that the process used for selecting the preferred option was robust and that the option of doing nothing has been considered

- Check that the preferred delivery option meets organizational and departmental objectives and standards

- Confirm that assumptions and dependencies (both internal and external) affecting the project have been identified and assessed

- Check if there is an opportunity to integrate the project with any other project or program

- Establish that the project organization has been considered and there is an overall project management process in place

Stakeholders

All of the project stakeholders should have been identified and their needs established and understood. The review should confirm that the stakeholders support the preferred option, including the recommended delivery approach and methods.

Risk Management

Confirm that there are suitable processes in place to identify, assess and manage current, anticipated and emerging risks:

- The risks for each of the options have been evaluated and the risks for the preferred option have been fully assessed

- Opportunities for risk transfer have been considered

- Risk management costs and time implications have been included in the cost and time estimate or as a contingency

- If the project is large, innovative or plans to use cutting-edge technology this has been considered in the risks along with the option of decomposing the project into sub-projects

Readiness for Next Stage

Finally the assessment should consider if the project is ready to move on to the next stage. The review should establish that:

- There is a realistic plan and schedule in place for the next stage of the project, which takes account of statutory and approval lead times

- There is a project organization in place for the next stage of the project with agreed roles and responsibilities, and the necessary resources are available at the right time, with the required skills and any necessary training is planned

- There is an up-to-date operational risk log in place

The assessment review should be planned, carried out and documented in the same way as for strategic investment review.

The assessment review process and production of a status report were set out on page 163.

Delivery Strategy

Gateway 2: delivery strategy is the second review of a stand alone project or a constituent project of a program. The purpose of the review is to confirm that the planned approach to deliver the solution meets the business needs, is affordable and achievable and is likely to achieve value for money. It also confirms that the project is ready to move ahead to the next stage.

Delivery Approach

The business requirements specification sets out how the business requirements for the project should be met. It should:

- Confirm that all options (internal and external) for delivering the required solution have been evaluated

- Assess if the client fully understands the business objectives and if the suppliers are likely to understand them

- Confirm that the project deliverables are accurately reflected in the requirement specification and that the project team have complied with all relevant policies and guidelines

- If it is a procurement approach, confirm that the selected procurement strategy has been defined and endorsed and that there is an adequate knowledge of potential suppliers

- Check that any factors that could impact on the procurement strategy have been addressed

- Confirm that the procurement approach will facilitate communication and cooperation between all parties and any other related projects and programs

Business Case

There is again a focus on the business case in this review to confirm that it is still sound now that the proposed approach to delivering the project has been defined. It should:

- Confirm that the business case continues to demonstrate business needs and contributes to the organization's strategy

- Establish that the projected costs are within budget and that the key stakeholders support the project

- Confirm that the organization is realistic about its ability to achieve a successful outcome

- Confirm that there is a clear definition of the total project scope

- Establish that the risks and issues relating to the business change are understood and there is a plan to address these

- Confirm that the stakeholders support the project and that the organization is fully committed to it

- Confirm that the stakeholders agree with and understand the benefits of the project and there is a benefits realization plan in place for evaluating the benefits

Risk Management

The review needs to confirm there are adequate plans in place for risk and issue management. It should:

- Establish that major risks and issues have been identified, understood, evaluated and taken into consideration in determining the delivery strategy

- Confirm that there are risk management plans in place

- Confirm that all issues raised have been or are being resolved

Current Stage Review

The current state of the project needs to be reviewed to establish that it is under control and that the reasons for any deviations have been established together with any necessary actions to prevent recurrence in future stages. A check should be made that any assumptions which were made at earlier reviews have now been verified.

Readiness for Next Stage

To confirm that there is a realistic project plan in place for the remaining stages by:

- Establishing that the schedule is reasonable and achievable and compliant with relevant policies and guidelines

- Confirm that the activities for the next stage of the project have been defined and allocated

- Confirming that the project has the necessary resources with appropriate skills and experience

The assessment review process and production of a status report were set out on page 163.

Investment Decision

Gateway 3: investment decision is the third review of a project. It will follow supplier selection for an external project or detailed analysis for an internal project. In either event, firm costs for the remainder of the project should now have been established. The purpose of this review is to confirm that the project is affordable and achievable, and is ready to move ahead to the next stage.

Solution Assessment

The proposed solution is reviewed to ensure that it meets the business needs and organizational and departmental objectives. It should confirm:

- If the suppliers (internal or external) have proposed any alternatives or options beyond the requirements specification and if so these have been assessed

- The proposed solution will deliver the business need described in the business case or if the proposed solution has affected the strategy or business benefits these have been evaluated and the proposed solution is still within budget

- The client and supplier are prepared for the development, implementation, transition and operation of any new services

- Any technical implications of the proposed solution have been assessed

- The project and the business have resources available with the appropriate skills and experience to achieve the intended outcomes

Business Case

The business case needs to be reviewed to confirm the project is still justified now the full costs have been established:

- Confirm that the project is still required and the proposed way forward fully meets the business need or if the decision requires the business case to be amended

- Establish that the most appropriate option has been selected, that the business case still demonstrates affordability and that the proposed solution represents good value for money

- Confirm that the client is realistic about their ability to manage the change

- Check that there is an agreed plan for the realization of anticipated benefits

- Confirm that suitable stakeholders, business and user representatives have been involved and have approved the proposed solution (and draft contracts if relevant)

Risk Management

The review should confirm that risk and issue management plans are up-to-date; all major risks and issues from this stage have been resolved; arrangements are in place to minimize risks to the business in the event of major problems during implementation; and any contracts reflect the standard terms and conditions and the required level of risk transfer.

Current Stage Review

The current state of the project needs to be reviewed to establish that it is under control and that the reasons for any deviations have been established, together with any necessary actions to prevent recurrence in future stages. Also, to confirm that any assumptions made at earlier reviews have been verified and that required departmental procurement, technical procedures and processes have been followed.

Readiness for Next Stage

Confirm that the working relationship between client and supplier is likely to succeed and that:

- All resources and internal funds are in place

- The supplier's project, risk and management plans are adequate and realistic

- The client's plan reflects the supplier's plan, and vice versa

- The long-term contract, administration plan and performance measurement processes are complete

- All mechanisms and processes are in place for the next stage

- The service management plan, administration and service level arrangements are complete

- There is an acceptance or commissioning strategy and an implementation strategy

Don't forget

The assessment review process and production of a status report were set out on page 163.

Readiness for Service

Gateway 4: readiness for service is the fourth review of a project. It will follow supplier appointment for an external project or authority to proceed for an internal project. In either event, the solution should now have been developed and be ready for implementation. The purpose of this review is to confirm that the developed solution is ready to be implemented.

Solution Readiness

The purpose of this review is to ensure that the developed solution is ready for implementation and that the business is ready to implement it. It should confirm that:

- Commissioning plans have been developed and are in line with the organization's policy and industry best practice

- The commissioning plans identify and address key areas such as communications, training, the commissioning period and confirm that all necessary testing has been performed to the end user's satisfaction

- The project SRO is ready to approve implementation

- There are feasible and tested contingency and reversion (back-out) arrangements in place

Business Case

The business case needs to be reviewed to confirm that the project is still required and the business case is still valid:

- Confirm that the project is still required and still meets the business needs and objectives of the relevant users and stakeholders

- Confirm that the business case is still valid

- If there have been any changes between the award of contract and completion of testing that affect the business change, confirm they have been reflected in the business case

- Confirm that the organization is ready for the business change and that it can implement the new services and maintain existing services

- Confirm there are appropriately skilled and experienced human resources available

Current Stage Review

The current state of the project needs to be reviewed to establish that it is under control and that the reasons for any deviations have been established. Confirm that:

- The delivered service meets all acceptance criteria

- The project is on track and running to plan and budget

- All stakeholder issues have been addressed

- All testing and commissioning, acceptance and transition procedures are complete

- All parties have accepted the commissioning or test results and any required action plans

- There are workable and tested contingency and reversion plans for implementation and operation

- The client and supplier have agreed on the implementation plans, including management of change, migration and data transfer, client and supplier implementation and roll-out

- The impact of any changes to the contract have been forecast, recorded and approved and the contract has been effectively managed and enforced

- There is a training plan and curriculum and they are ready for implementation

Risk Management

The review should confirm that the risk and issue management plans are up-to-date and any risks and issues from the contract award and implementation plan have been properly managed. If there are any unresolved issues, the risks of implementing rather than delaying, pending resolution, have been considered.

Readiness for Next Stage

Confirm all project elements are ready for service; the client is ready for the new ways of working; any contract management process is in place; a process is in place to manage performance; a process is in place to measure and report benefits; ongoing operation and maintenance arrangements are in place and there is a process in place for post-implementation reviews.

The assessment review process and production of a status report were set out on page 163.

171

Benefits Realization

Gateway 5: benefits realization is the fifth review of a project and will follow the implementation of the project solution. The solution should now be up and running and the purpose of this review is to assess whether the business case for the project was realistic and benefits have started to accrue in line with it.

Operational Review

The implemented solution needs to be reviewed in its operational environment to ascertain if:

- The service or facility is operating as specified and change management, risk management and relationship management are effective

- Training and support is adequate and the training material and program have been delivered and are kept up-to-date

- Governance and contractual relationships are satisfactory and there are plans for continued contract management

Business Case

Confirm that in the light of the implemented and operational solution, that the business case is still valid:

- Confirm if the business benefits, as set out in the business case and benefit management plan, have been realized and the users are satisfied with the operational service

- Establish if the needs of the business, stakeholders or end users have changed

- Confirm that all governance and stakeholder issues have been addressed, including: the statutory process, communications, external relations, environmental issues and personnel

Plans for Ongoing Improvements

Establish what scope there is for ongoing improvements in value for money and performance:

- Ascertain if more could be done for less cost, the supplier could deliver a better service for the same price or maintenance costs could be reduced

- Check if the organization has benchmarked its processes by comparing them with other similar organizations

- Check that the organization is setting realistic targets for continuous improvement from this service and if the client and supplier are working together to identify opportunities for improvement through innovation

- Check if the organization has performance assessments to cover all aspects of the contract and whether these demonstrate evidence of success against an existing baseline

Organizational Maturity

Review the organizational learning and maturity targets:

- Check if the organization has implemented an effective process for identifying lessons learned, applying them and sharing them across the organization

- Check if there has been a review of how well the project was managed and that the results have been fed back to the organization for refinement of processes and feedback to future projects

- Check if suppliers are encouraged to learn from experience

Future Readiness

Plans for further service provision:

- Establish if there is an ongoing need for further provision of this service and if so its likely scope

- Establish if there are any major issues with the current contract (such as confidence in or the flexibility of the supplier) that could affect the approach to re-tendering for the service in future

- Establish if re-tendering will be straightforward or if there is a danger that the client is now locked in

- Ascertain if agreements have been made to ensure a smooth hand over at the end of the contract

- Ascertain what the predicted condition of any assets will be at the end of the contract period

Gateway five may be repeated as necessary until full benefits realization is completed.

Don't forget

The assessment review process and production of a status report were set out on page 163.

Summary

- The gateway review process is based on the use of short peer reviews of projects and programs to highlight any risks and issues which could threaten the ultimate success of the program or project

- While the process can be applied to any project, it is most beneficial on larger projects and programs

- The process consists of six gateways, usually numbered from zero to five (but sometimes from one to six)

- **Gateway 0: Strategic Assessment** only applies to programs and is carried out at various phases to establish the continuing viability of the program. Each of the constituent projects are then reviewed using the other five gateways

- **Gateway 1: Business Justification** is carried out at the end of the initiation stage of a project to confirm that the business case is sound

- **Gateway 2: Delivery Strategy** is carried out at the end of the second stage in a project once the strategy for meeting the business case has been specified

- **Gateway 3: Investment Decision** is carried out after the third stage of a project before any major purchase, contract or start of an in-house development

- **Gateway 4: Readiness for Service** is carried out just before the implementation stage of a project to confirm that the delivered solution is fit for purpose prior to going operational

- **Gateway 5: Benefits Evaluation** is carried out one or more times during the operational stage of a project and prior to decommissioning the delivered solution to establish the benefits realization of the delivered solution

- Each of the reviews concentrates on one aspect of the program or project but also confirms that the business case is still valid

- At the end of each review a report is issued flagging any issues or recommendations using a red, amber and green traffic signal to illustrate the criticality of the item

11 Action Plan

This chapter sets out a road map and summarizes the steps required to implement project, program and portfolio management.

Hot tip

Whatever else you do or don't do, make sure you carry out these first two steps if you have not already done so.

Hot tip

A set of checklists for implementing project, program and portfolio management is available on our website. Go to **www.ineasysteps. com/resource-centre/ downloads/**

Road Map

This final chapter brings together all the processes required to implement successful project, program and portfolio management in any organization. The road map is illustrated opposite and the necessary steps to implement it are:

1 Define a standard organizational approach to project management (life cycle and supporting processes) and gain agreement to it in the organization

2 Set up a project office to manage the documentation of the standard approach and provide support and training to project managers

3 Define a standard approach to program management (life cycle and supporting processes) and gain agreement to it in the organization

4 Set up a program office (possibly based on the project office) to manage the program documentation and provide support to program managers

5 Define a standard approach to gateway reviews and gain agreement to it in the organization

6 Add the responsibility for organizing gateway reviews to the program office

7 Define a standard approach to portfolio management (life cycle and supporting processes) and gain agreement to it in the organization

8 Set up a portfolio office (possibly based on the program office) to manage and support the processes

Use these guidelines to develop your own road map, starting from where your organization is today and ending up where you want to be in the future. This will be a fairly major project in its own right and each step will take some time to achieve. So set realistic targets and review your progress regularly.

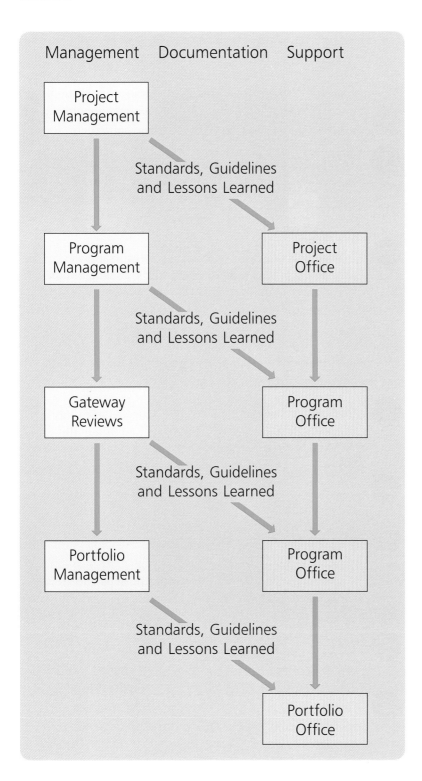

Project Management

The starting point for the introduction of project, program and portfolio management is with project management as everything else builds on this. The following steps start from the basis that the organization is currently at level one; if your organization is more mature than this just tick off the steps that are already implemented until you reach one that isn't and start there:

1 Define and document a standard project life cycle (use the example on page 30 as a starting point) but be sure to add the rider that stages can be added or removed and the stage names can be changed if appropriate

2 Involve all project managers in the organization to get their input and agreement to the standard, obtain management approval and issue the standard life cycle with guidelines on its use

Once you have completed these first two steps you are at project management maturity level 2: Repeatable. The next steps are to produce the supporting methodology:

3 Define and document the project management processes to support the project life cycle based on an off-the-shelf methodology such as PMBOK, PRINCE or EPM

4 Again, involve all project managers in the organization in the process and get their agreement, management approval and issue the standard methodology and guidelines on its use

Once you have completed all four of the above steps you are at project management maturity level 3: Defined. The next steps are to set up a project office and project reporting:

5 Set up a project office (as described on page 35) and transfer the documented standards and guidelines to it

6 Institute regular review meetings between the project office and project managers to revise and update the standards based on experience

Hot tip

EPM (Effective Project Management in easy steps) provides a simple and effective project life cycle and supporting processes. PRINCE and PMBOK provide more detailed methodologies.

Don't forget

The project office only needs to be one person (possibly only part time) to start with.

Define and document a standard project management reporting process including a definition of the metrics that you will use to track the success of projects

Reporting and Metrics

Most project management methodologies (including the three mentioned in step 3 opposite) include standard report structures and suggested metrics. These need to be standardized across all projects and include metrics on time, cost (including human resource cost) and functionality delivered. They should enable the three basic questions to be asked: is the project on time, is it to budget, and will it deliver all the required functionality?

This information should already be recorded in each project; now it needs to be reported to the project office so that it can record the metrics and track project performance.

Once you have completed these seven steps you are at project management maturity level 4: Managed. You could choose to stop at this point and move onto program management but the remaining steps are relatively straightforward and are really just about delegation and empowerment.

Process Improvement

The project office has (in steps 6 and 7) the mechanism it needs to obtain and record the necessary performance data. The following two steps will complete the process:

8 Discuss with the project office staff how they will use the data they are collecting on an ongoing basis to refine the standards and guidelines and ask them to document the processes they plan to use

9 Agree these new processes with the project office and project managers, hand over to them to continue going forward and add it to their responsibilities

Once these final two steps have been implemented you are at project management maturity level 5: Optimizing. The process is now run by the project office and you can move onto the next stage of the process, program management.

If you are not planning to implement program management you don't need to carry out these steps. However, you should make sure there is an awareness of program management (as covered on page 87).

Both the SPM and MSP methodologies were described on page 39.

Program Management

Having reached a project management maturity level of managed (level 4) or optimizing (level 5) you are ready for the second stage of the journey, implementing program management. The following steps start from the basis that the organization is currently at program management maturity level one (initial), if your organization is more mature than this just tick off the steps that are already implemented until you reach one that isn't:

1 Define and document a standard program life cycle (use the example on page 50 as a starting point) but note that names can be changed if appropriate and stages added

2 Involve all project and program managers in the organization to get their input and agreement to the standard, obtain management approval and issue the standard life cycle with guidelines on its use

Once you have completed these first two steps you are at program management maturity level 2: Repeatable. The next steps are to produce the supporting methodology and processes:

3 Define and document the program management processes to support the program life cycle (possibly based on an off-the-shelf methodology such as SPM or MSP)

4 Again, involve all of the organization's project and program managers in the process and get their agreement, management approval and issue the standard methodology and guidelines on its use

Once you have completed all four of the above steps you are at program management maturity level 3: Defined. The next steps are to set up a program office and program reporting:

5 Set up a program office (as described on page 57) and transfer the documented standards and guidelines to it

6 Institute regular review meetings between the program office and program and project managers to revise and update the standards based on experience

Define and document a standard program management reporting process including a definition of the metrics that you will use to track the success of programs

Reporting and Metrics

Most program management methodologies (including those mentioned in step 3 opposite) include standard reports and suggested metrics. These need to be standardized across all programs and include the prime metrics of benefits management and strategic alignment. Essentially, the metrics should enable two basic questions to be asked: is the program still aligned with corporate strategy and is it delivering the projected benefits?

This information should be recorded in each program and reported to the program office so that they can record the metrics and track program performance.

Once you have completed these seven steps you are at program management maturity level 4: Managed. You could choose to stop at this point and move on to gateway reviews, but the remaining steps are relatively straightforward and are really just about delegation and empowerment.

Process Improvement

The program office has (in steps 6 and 7) the mechanism it needs to obtain and record the necessary performance data. The following two steps will complete the process:

8 Discuss with the program office staff how they will use the data they are collecting on an ongoing basis to refine the standards and guidelines and ask them to document the processes they plan to use

9 Agree these new processes with the program managers and program office, hand over to them to continue going forward and add it to their responsibilities

Once these final two steps have been implemented you are at program management maturity level 5: Optimizing. The process is now run by the program office and you can move on to the next stage of the process, gateway reviews.

Gateway Reviews

Having reached a program management maturity level of managed (level 4) or optimizing (level 5) you are ready for the next stage of the journey, implementing gateway reviews. While not an essential element of project, program and portfolio management, they are a very effective form of program and project governance.

Gateway reviews can be implemented using the following steps:

1 Define and document a high level gateway review process based on your program and project life cycles and the introduction and overview diagrams (pages 158 to 161) in the previous chapter

2 Involve all project and program managers in the organization to get their input and agreement to the process, obtain management approval and issue the standard life cycle with guidelines on its use

3 Define and document the remainder of the gateway review process based on an off-the-shelf methodology such as the OGC Gateway process or the remainder of the previous chapter (pages 162 to 173)

4 In discussion with all interested parties develop guidelines on when the gateway review process must be used, when it can be used and when it should not be used (on very small or low budget projects for example)

5 Again, involve all project and program managers in the organization in the process, get their agreement, obtain management approval and issue the standard methodology and guidelines on its use

6 Transfer the documented standards and guidelines to the program office and institute regular review meetings between the program office and program and project managers to revise and update the standards and guidelines based on experience

Don't forget

If required, you can develop a mini review process for smaller projects.

7 Select a pilot program or large project on which to introduce the gateway review process and gain the agreement of the senior responsible owner, program or project board as appropriate. This does not have to be a new program or project as the gateway review process can be started at any phase or stage of a program or project

8 Identify and select an initial group of potential peer reviewers with a range of skills that are relevant for the pilot program or project and give them appropriate training in the gateway review process

A short workshop should be sufficient to introduce the process.

9 Review the results of the pilot program or project gateway reviews with the program office and the pilot program and project managers. The program office should use these reviews to revise and refine the gateway review processes and standards

Roll Out the Process

On completion of the pilot, and once all involved are happy with the process, standards and guidelines, it should be rolled out:

10 Obtain senior management agreement to the roll out of the process, standards and guidelines

11 Work with the program office to plan and implement the roll out to all relevant existing programs and projects and all future relevant programs and projects

12 Work with the program office to identify and select further potential peer reviewers

If you are not implementing program management, then work with the project office in place of the program office.

13 Hand over final responsibility for the gateway review process to the program office

The gateway review process is now operational in the organization, administered and supported by the program office. It should continue to develop and enhance the process based on further feedback from each new program and project.

Portfolio Management

Having reached a project (and program if applicable) management maturity level of managed (level 4) or optimizing (level 5) you are ready for the final stage of the journey: implementing portfolio management. The following steps start from the basis that the organization is currently at portfolio management maturity level one (initial), if your organization is more mature just tick off the steps that are implemented until you reach one that isn't:

1 Define and document a standard portfolio life cycle (use the example on page 70 as a starting point) but note that names can be changed if appropriate and process groups and processes added

2 Set up a central project database to allow projects to be ranked, obtain management approval and issue the standard life cycle with guidelines on its use

Once you have completed these first two steps you are at portfolio management maturity level 2: Repeatable. The next steps are to produce the supporting methodology and processes:

3 Define and document the portfolio management processes to support the program life cycle based (if required) on an off-the-shelf methodology such as SPM or MoP

4 Ensure that projects are ranked on a return on investment (or other appropriate measure) basis and the portfolio is maximized on a value for money basis, issue the standard methodology and guidelines on its use

Once you have completed all four of the above steps you are at portfolio management maturity level 3: Defined. The next steps are to set up a portfolio office and portfolio reporting:

5 Set up a portfolio office (as described on page 75) and transfer the documented standards and guidelines to it

6 Institute regular review meetings between the portfolio office and the portfolio, program and project managers to revise and update the standards based on experience

Don't forget

Both the SPM and MoP methodologies were described on pages 66 to 69.

7 Define and document a standard portfolio management reporting process including a definition of the metrics that will be used to track the success of the portfolio

Reporting and Metrics

The two portfolio management methodologies (mentioned in step 3 opposite) include reporting and metrics as part of portfolio governance. The main aim of portfolio management is to maximize the value of the portfolio, align it to the strategy of the organization and to balance the portfolio to make best use of human and financial resources.

Metrics should focus on the value of the portfolio and the benefits realized but they also need to gather data on human and financial resource usage. Senior management want to know that the portfolio is aligned with corporate strategy, is realizing the projected benefits and making the best use of resources. This information should be reported to the portfolio office so that it can record the metrics and track portfolio performance.

Once you have completed these seven steps you are at portfolio management maturity level 4: Managed. You could choose to stop at this point but the remaining steps are relatively straightforward.

Process Improvement

The program office has (in steps 6 and 7) the mechanism it needs to obtain and record the necessary performance data. The following two steps will complete the process:

8 Discuss with the portfolio office staff how they will use the collected data to refine the standards and guidelines for continuous process improvement and ask them to document the processes they plan to use

9 Agree these new processes with the portfolio manager and hand them over to the portfolio office

Once these final two steps have been implemented you are at portfolio management maturity level 5: Optimizing. The process is now run by the portfolio office and your work is done.

Summary

- Develop a road map from where the organization currently is to where you want to get to

- Project management is the starting point from which everything else builds; define and document a project life cycle, supporting processes and guidance; obtain agreement and issue them

- Set up a project office to provide support to all project managers and transfer the processes and guidelines to it

- Institute regular reviews between the project office and project managers and transfer continuous process improvement responsibility to it

- Define and document a program management life cycle, supporting processes and guidance; obtain agreement to and issue them

- Develop a program office to provide support to the program managers and transfer the processes and guidance to it

- Institute regular reviews between the program office and program managers and transfer continuous process improvement responsibility to it

- Define and document gateway review processes, obtain agreement to and issue them

- Transfer the gateway review processes to the program office, train peer reviewers, carry out a pilot and refine the processes; then roll the processes out to all programs and large projects

- Define and document a portfolio management life cycle with supporting processes and guidance, obtain agreement and issue them

- Set up a central project database to hold relevant data for the portfolio and use it to evaluate projects

- Develop a portfolio office to provide support to the portfolio manager and transfer the processes and guidance to it

- Congratulations, you have reached the end of the journey and project, program and portfolio management are implemented

Index

P

Q

R